THE OLD-FASHIONED

THE OLD-FASHIONED

THE STORY OF THE
WORLD'S FIRST CLASSIC COCKTAIL,
WITH RECIPES AND LORE

Robert Simonson

Photographs by Daniel Krieger

TEN SPEED PRESS
Berkeley

Published in the United States by Ten Speed Press,
an imprint of the Crown Publishing Group, a division
of Random House LLC, a Penguin Random House
Company, New York.
www.crownpublishing.com
www.tenspeed.com

Ten Speed Press and the Ten Speed Press colophon
are registered trademarks of Random House LLC

Library of Congress Cataloging-in-Publication Data
Simonson, Robert.
The old-fashioned : the story of the world's first classic
cocktail, with recipes and lore / Robert Simonson.
   pages cm
Includes index.
1. Cocktails—History. 2. Bitters—History. I. Title.
TX951.S5835 2014
  641.87'4—dc23
2013037239

Hardcover ISBN: 978-1-60774-535-8
eBook ISBN: 978-1-60774-536-5

Printed in China

Design by Katy Brown

13

First Edition

To Doris June Pommerening Simonson,
Old-Fashioned drinker

PREFACE

"I never treated it as just a cocktail."
—DORIS SIMONSON

MY MOTHER NEVER DRANK LIQUOR until she was twenty-one. She followed the rules. But when she embarked on what would become a long drinking life, she did so with purpose and not a little forethought.

The first order of business was to find her drink. In those post–World War II days, when the cocktail hour was as inviolable a part of any day as sunrise and sunset, one had one's drink. There was none of this flitting about from cocktail to cocktail. You found a mix that delighted the palate and soothed the mind in the right proportions and stuck by it.

She began with Manhattans. She liked the way they looked, shining like liquid embers inside a long-stemmed glass. But, after a while, they gave her headaches, which she blamed on the sweet vermouth. (Vermouth is ever the scapegoat.) She then tried Martinis, but found them daunting and dangerous. Finally, she found her level in the Old-Fashioned. Some of her reasoning was spurious. She'd ask for as much accompanying fruit as the bar could furnish as well as a healthy spurt of soda water, because, "even in those days, watching your weight was important." But the remainder of her logic is hard to fault.

"A lot depends on why you're having an Old-Fashioned," she said, some sixty years after she sampled her first. "If you're having one as a drink in the evening, you'd probably rather have a strong one, because you're not going to have two Old-Fashioneds. If you're at somebody's home or visiting with people, it's never just a cocktail. I never treated it as just a cocktail. To me, a cocktail was an avenue to socializing. Everyone did it. It was something we did while we were visiting and laughing and singing and talking. It was a tool to meet people and relax.

"I treated it as an all-purpose drink. I never went through this thing where you say, 'Oh, it's before dinner, so we need a before-dinner drink; or, it's dinner, so we want something light; or it's after dinner, etc.' It was something I enjoyed drinking, and I could control what I wanted by telling the bartender not to put too much liquor in it, or to put a lot of fruit in it. You could almost make up the recipe for your Old-Fashioned.

"You find people's personalities coming out in Old-Fashioneds. A lot of men will drink Old-Fashioneds, but they will tell the bartender, in no uncertain terms, 'Very little, if anything, mixed in.' Mostly, it turned out what they wanted was a bourbon on the rocks. They basically wanted a nice strong drink with plenty of ice cubes, so as it sat there it became a little more mellow. Whereas women basically wanted all the things that went with it."

"And," she concluded, "it's so beautiful to look at."

1

THE STORY

"THE GRANDFATHER OF THEM ALL"

NOVELIST KINGSLEY AMIS called it "the only cocktail really to rival the martini and its variants." His countryman, writer Alec Waugh, considered a bourbon Old-Fashioned or a very dry five-to-one Martini "the best preludes to a good dinner." James Beard, the American culinary godfather, named a dry Martini, a dry Daiquiri, and "an old-fashioned without any refuse in the way of fruit" the best of cocktails. Drama critic and cultural arbiter George Jean Nathan deemed the Martini, Manhattan, and Old-Fashioned "the inaugural cocktail trinity." "The grandfather of them all," decreed newspaperman nonpareil H. L. Mencken.

The Martini and Manhattan have long been recognized as owning space atop the Mount Olympus of classic cocktails. But, not too long ago, the Old-Fashioned's footing on that mountain was shaky. Once an austere, perfectly balanced assemblage of whiskey, bitters, sugar, and water—a cocktail at its most elemental—it had taken on several decades' worth of baggage. Those few who still ordered it in the waning decades of the twentieth century were handed a potion adulterated with cherries, orange slices, and soda, and made with weak whiskey and weaker ice.

Citizens who came of drinking age around the turn of the new millennium would have been hard-pressed to understand why intellectual leaders of the last century—normally busy mulling headier matters—had taken time out of their day to signal praise for what seemed an exceedingly silly, unsophisticated drink. The Old-Fashioned? That tarted-up fruit salad slopped together at supper clubs and musty old saloons? That sickly sweet, imprecise concoction that, only by the most charitable stretch of imagination, could be called a whiskey drink? The Martini, another relic from parental cocktail hours of the Eisenhower years, at least retained some vestigial dignity, standing cold and clear in its sleek signature glass. But the Old-Fashioned had not weathered the years at all well. It looked like an adult version of a kiddie cocktail and seemed as stodgy and backward as its name.

Fortunes reversed sharply for the unlucky Old-Fashioned only a handful of years ago, when a few keen-eyed mixologists and armchair drink historians spied the outline of the cocktail's true soul hiding behind all that sacchariferous window dressing. Remove the muddled fruit, the seltzer, the 7-Up, the sour mix, the taillight-red cherry; switch out the bottom-shelf rotgut for some quality whiskey; replace the industrial "cheater ice" (that is, basic bar ice, small and quick to melt) with a single crystalline cube, and—voilà!—you have something very near (identical, actually) to the earliest Old-Fashioneds from the pre-Prohibition era.

But more than that, you have a drink that very closely matches the original definition of the word "cocktail," period. The earliest known printed definition of the word appeared in the newspaper the *Balance and Columbian Repository* in 1806: "A stimulating liquor, composed of spirits of any kind, sugar, water, and bitters." That formula is precisely what lies at the heart of the Old-Fashioned, with bourbon or rye being the spirit and Angostura the preferred bitters.

The Old-Fashioned, then, is in form the primordial cocktail, and one with a far older pedigree than the Martini or Manhattan. Having gleaned this truth, mixologists (that fanciful title, too, dates from the nineteenth century) reached for their knives and hacked away the modern moss that had accumulated around the forgotten classic. And, in short order, the Old-Fashioned was restored to its elemental state, which it had not widely enjoyed in a century.

Here is a drink where both the flavor and color of the base spirit shines. When properly made according to its original specifications, the Old-Fashioned's amber glow is no longer obscured by phosphorescent refugees from the produce department. The biting edge of the whiskey is not dulled by corn syrup but instead gently softened by a touch of water, sweetened by a lump of sugar, and accented by the bitters, which bind together the drink's few ingredients in harmony. Chilled and anchored by a single large cube of ice, the drink is at home in its low-slung, eponymous glass. As the cube slowly melts, the potion incrementally alters, calming, over time, both itself and its owner. This is a drink to be lingered over, a drink made for contemplation.

By the end of 2009 or so, the Old-Fashioned had taken pride of place atop the menus at not only the best cocktail bars in the United States, but also restaurants and hotel bars. At many, it became what it had not been in an age: the bar's top-selling drink. And your mother or grandfather was no longer the one ordering it. You were. It was indeed, as George Jean Nathan said, a member of the "cocktail trinity," even though it was the last to be recognized as a member of the triumvirate.

FIRST, THE WHISKEY COCKTAIL

THE OLD-FASHIONED'S REDEMPTION was long in coming. No cocktail has endured the same roller-coaster ride of reputation. It has had every sling and arrow of barroom fashion thrown at it. That will happen when a drink—nearly alone among its brothers— sticks around for two centuries, never having completely fallen out of favor, and having avoided being crushed under the wheel of progress called Prohibition. Once a simple assemblage of whiskey, sugar, and bitters, restless bartenders have dashed into it absinthe, curaçao, maraschino liqueur—all fancy liqueurs that found their place on the backbar in the mid-nineteenth century. It's been a fruit salad, with lemon, orange, cherry, and pineapple piled high atop its rim to delight the eye of the decadent Gilded Age tipplers. Later, sometime after Prohibition, the fruit sunk to the bottom in a muddled mess. It's been shellacked with seltzer, sour mix, and lemon-lime soda, and made with rye, bourbon, and brandy. It is a drink that raises the hackles of its devotees, each generation decrying the cocktail that the younger generation embraces as an Old-Fashioned as being nothing of the sort. It's a drink with a history so divisive that—alone among major cocktails—it has sailed under two different names.

The name on its birth certificate was Whiskey Cocktail. The moniker said it all: it was a cocktail (according to the technical definition cited above—spirit, sugar, bitters, water) made of whiskey. It was first mentioned in a book in 1862, when Jerry Thomas secured his place in cocktail history by becoming the first bartender to collect and publish the drink recipes of his time. He defined a Whiskey Cocktail as a couple dashes of Boker's bitters (a brand of bitters popular throughout much of the nineteenth century before it was felled by Prohibition), twice as many dashes of gum syrup (a complex form of sugar syrup made with gum arabic, which is a type of tree resin), and a "wine-glass" of whiskey. This mixture was shaken over fine ice, strained into a "fancy red wine-glass," and topped with a twist of lemon. His definition of the drink is fairly consistent with other accounts of the time; in 1873, the newspaper the *Brooklyn Eagle* defined the Whiskey Cocktail as "a sort of cross between a plain glass of whisky, a bottle of bitters and a drop of lemon juice."

Mentions of Whiskey Cocktails began appearing in newspapers in the early nineteenth century, though whiskey was not a major player in the cocktail world at the time. Brandy, Holland (also known as Dutch) gin, sherry, and rum all loomed larger as base spirits. Among cocktails, the Mint Julep, Brandy Smash, Sherry

Cobbler, and Gin Cocktail (basically an Old-Fashioned made with Dutch gin) far outpaced the Whiskey Cocktail in sales and status. But the drink picked up popularity as the century wore on and peripatetic Americans became more familiar with America's native liquors. In 1859, the *Memphis Daily Appeal* called the Whiskey Cocktail a "fashionable accompaniment" to the sporting life, along with smoking cigars, chewing tobacco, and playing poker.

The Whiskey Cocktail was prevalent enough in the middle decades of the nineteenth century for it to be made in large batches and sold as provisions to the Union army during the Civil War. Officers liked their fix as well. General Philip Sheridan—a man who enjoyed good drink—testified that Civil War general and Gettysburg hero Winfield Scott Hancock possessed the finest hand in the Union army at compounding the drink. Even the war's chief villain, actor and assassin John Wilkes Booth, is said to have dulled the pain of existence through "the continuous consumption of whiskey cocktails."

During these early years of its prominence, the drink was widely regarded as a "matutinal cocktail"—that is, you drank it in the morning. (For reasons that need no explanation, this expression has fallen out of use.) A man of firm mind, but infirm stomach and head, made the local tavern his first stop of the day. There he ordered an eye opener. The *Brooklyn Eagle* reported in 1881 that, as a "bracer up," the cocktail was much preferred by "the Brooklyn boys." An 1874 piece of advice from the *Indiana Progress* in Pennsylvania had it that "a bourbon whiskey cocktail before breakfast is the best thing for complexion."

"Cocktails are sought after in the morning," said William Schmidt, a bartender-sage of the late nineteenth century. "To make a good one you must fill a goblet with fine ice, add two dashes of Angostura bitters, three dashes of gum and one of absinthe, and a small drink of whiskey or other liquor; shake well and squeeze a lemon peel over the top—don't drop it in—and serve." Schmidt was, of course, prescribing a Whiskey Cocktail. (The addition of absinthe made it an "improved" Whiskey Cocktail, but more on that in a moment.)

By 1882, the Whiskey Cocktail was so popular that it engendered a political scandal. Members of the House of Representatives attending President Garfield's funeral train were chastised in print for spending "$1,700 for liquors, wines, and lunches . . . $300 being for 'whiskey cocktails' alone."

By then, however, Whiskey Cocktails were not what they once had been. The fluctuations in profile for which the drink would become known had already begun. Whiskey Cocktails were "improved," as the mixologist terminology went. Bartenders were fascinated by the wealth of European liqueurs and elixirs reaching American shores. Some of these, notably vermouth, led to the creation of fine new cocktails. But for cocktails that already had been invented, the expanded backbar led to experimentation and the adulteration of time-tested formulas. Whiskey Cocktail recipes began to call for a bit of absinthe, a drop of curaçao, a touch of maraschino, or all three. Purists observed with horror.

THE REBELLION

THE HISTORY OF THE COCKTAIL is one of advancement and correction, fashion and backlash. As soon as a new mixing method or ingredient surfaces, the restlessly curious bartending community has at it, turning out newfangled creations until the barroom standard-bearers cry "Hold!" Such is the story of the advent of the Old-Fashioned—the cocktail, its method, and its name.

Sometime in the late 1870s and early 1880s, principled drinkers began to decide that the "improved" cocktails being passed over the bar were not improvements at all. They were desecrations of beverages that had been better left alone. In an 1886 article in *Comment and Dramatic Times* titled "The Cocktail of To-Day," journalist, novelist, and playwright Leander Richardson laid out the dilemma. "The modern cocktail has come to be so complex a beverage that people are beginning to desert it," raged Richardson. He continued:

> A bartender in one of the most widely-known New York establishments for the dispensation of drinks was telling me the other day that there had set in an unmistakable stampede in favor of old-fashioned cocktails. In the regular line of drinks coming under this name every bartender seems to have established his own private brand, so that people who are in the habit of whetting their appetites by the use of the friendly cocktail never know beforehand what they are going to take into their stomachs as they pass from bar to bar. The old-fashioned cocktail, on the contrary, is nearly everywhere recognized as being made with a little sugar, a little bitters, a lump of ice, a piece of twisted lemon peel, and a good deal

of whisky. It has no absinthe, no chartreuse and no other flavoring extract injected into it, and if not poured in too heavily upon an empty stomach it is anything but unwholesome. It is, therefore, hardly a wonder that people are going back to it, after being surfeited with all kinds of mixtures that the active minds of bartenders can invent.

In a single, concise harangue, Richardson neatly delineated the new fashion for old-styled drinking. As he indicated in his complaint, his call for "old-fashioned cocktails" was being seconded by others. Soon enough the name would stick, moving from generic term to specific order.

It's tempting to say the Old-Fashioned was simply a back-to-basics continuation of the good old Whiskey Cocktail, a way for "the old boys" to "get their money's worth of whisky," as the *Anaconda Standard* put it in 1890. And certainly the short list of ingredients—spirit, sugar, water, bitters, twist—hadn't changed. But the method by which those agents were combined and presented had.

Newly directed in their roles were the sweetener and the ice. Older formulas for the Whiskey Cocktail nearly always called for simple syrup, gum syrup, or something similar (though it's likely there was a period before that when sugar rather than syrup was employed). In newer cocktail books and news accounts, however, the Old-Fashioned was made using raw (nonsyrup) sugar, which was wetted with water and bitters and then muddled. The Whiskey Cocktail as recorded by Jerry Thomas was stirred over ice and then strained into the glass. This new Old-Fashioned was pointedly served on the rocks. Or, rather, on one big rock. A large chunk of the stuff was specifically called for in many recipes.

In an 1883 *Chicago Tribune* story, a local barman explained that part of the attraction of the "very popular" Old-Fashioned cocktail was "there is only one lump of ice used in them, and very little mixing is done, so the liquor is not cut up as it is in the cracked ice used in the modern cocktail." The ice also had a decorative function. In his eponymous 1899 cocktail manual, John Applegreen instructed Old-Fashioned makers to "have lump ice about the size of an egg" on hand, "but cut square or diamond-shape, as this tends to improve the appearance very much in serving."

Customers noticed, and approved. In a contemporaneous article in the Wisconsin paper the *Marshfield Times*, a "Bright Young Man" boasts of his knowledge of the ways of Chicago bartenders:

> *It takes a big piece of ice to make an old-fashioned cocktail properly. For years the barkeepers have been content to break up ice in irregular shapes, making pieces about as big as a toy rubber ball, which are dropped into the soothing mixture. But Chicago bartenders have lately developed a taste in this little matter for ice cut into perfect cubes about two inches on a side, so that every cocktail gets just as much ice as every other one. Several large saloons have gone a step further and have the ice frozen to order in balls which fit nicely into a glass.*

Balls, blocks, and diamonds—the Old-Fashioned may be been simple, but it didn't lack glamour.

The insistence on ice in the drink can possibly be explained by the drink's long journey from quick knock-back to sipping cocktail. The Whiskey Cocktails of the early nineteenth century were not long for this world. They were served "up," without ice, and were drunk in haste. By 1867, however, drinking had become more leisurely. John Oxenford, a reporter sent by the *Liverpool Daily Post* to observe New York for two months, noted the change. "The ordinary whiskey cocktail," he wrote, "is composed of the spirit, a few lumps of ice, an infusion of bitters, and a particle of lemon, the whole drink not exceeding the cubic contents of a wine glass. Here, indeed, is the solution of the enigma that the Americans drink so often and yet are so rarely found in a state of disgusting inebriety. They are not great topers, but frequent sippers."

A "toper" (English slang for a heavy drinker) and a "sipper" are the main figures in a fable printed in an 1884 issue of the *New York Tribune*. The latter, a young sport, is nipping at fashionable Chartreuse, while the former, an old man, clutches "four fingers of tawny rye." The topic at hand: changing drinking habits. The elder expounds that his generation had barrooms, while the younger breed enjoy grand cafés like the Hoffman House. The past generation worked harder and had but little spare time to tipple; the younger had idle hours galore. "It was mighty quick work, I can tell you," asserted the ancient in the story.

We drank in those days, I can assure you. We dip not sip . . . We didn't waste anytime about it, either. Just stood up to the bar and drank our liquor down like men. Sometimes we downed it, and sometimes it downed us. . . . You young fellows have changed all that, and I'll tell you frankly that I think the change is for the better. We old fellows sneer and sniff about it, may be, but the change that has come over the drinking habits of New York has left us not so thoroughly American perhaps, but at any rate healthier and more respectable.

The two drinkers end their reverie with the older man calling for what is evidently the appropriate compromise drink, "one little old-fashioned cocktail." Plenty of whiskey, but made for leisure.

OF MUDDLERS AND SPOONS

THE TRANSFORMATION OF the Whiskey Cocktail into the Old-Fashioned was not just a return to simple drinking—no frills, no modifiers, just plain honest whiskey, honestly accentuated. It also seemed to stem from an insistence on every red-blooded American's right to have his drink built in unassailably democratic fashion.

In terms of construction, the Old-Fashioned was kept on a tight leash. Other, fancier cocktails involved who knows what sort of syrups. With an Old-Fashioned, however, there was no question. You saw the sugar muddled into sweet slush before your eyes. The wooden muddler and the drink were, in fact, so tied together in the public imagination that a pre-Prohibition report in the *St. Joseph Observer* comically suggested that "the forests hitherto felled for pestles to mash the lump sugar will [now] build great fleets."

At some bars, an Old-Fashioned drinker was allowed to pour the whiskey from bottle to glass himself, a practice that was already common when straight whiskey was ordered. Moreover, the cocktail was served in the same glass in which it was made. There was no elaborate transferring of liquid from one vessel to the next. This was yet another bit of simplification designed to flatter the imbiber's sense of control.

Further placing the drink in the customer's hands was the small silver spoon that was traditionally popped into every Old-Fashioned. The tradition, completely forgotten today, is an odd one in retrospect. But from the late nineteenth century through the advent of Prohibition, it was the norm. The phrase "Serve with spoon in glass" or something similar is seen in recipe after recipe from this period, making the Old-Fashioned one of the only American cocktails that had, as its garnish, a utensil. (Some bartenders were even freer with their spoons. Mixologist Harry Johnson, in his *Bartenders' Manual*, recommended giving a spoon to every customer should he want to scoop out the fruit from a cocktail without "putting his finger into the glass.")

The spoons were so common that the *Baltimore Sun* observed in 1934, "The gentleman's upper coat pocket was found invariably to contain one spoon for each of his old-fashioned cocktails." What were the spoons for? The same article argued that "a sensible man always uses the spoon to scrape out the deliciously flavored sugar which lingers in the bottom of the drained glass. Obviously, one does not use for that purpose a spoon which has been lying about on the bar."

Obviously. Obvious, too, to the writer was how one managed the trick of drinking from a glass that contained a protruding piece of metal.

One can't hold the spoon in the other hand, for the other hand must be free for a variety of purposes, such as an occasional easy gesture to explain a complex matter under discussion, or a hasty reach for one's watch to see how close the little woman at home probably is to the boiling point, or even a quick grab at the edge of the bar in a demonstration of tender regard. And if the spoon can't be held in the hand, or laid on the bar, admittedly there's no other place to put it save in the glass.

Those who did lay the spoon on the bar before drinking had "very bad manners."

What of the danger, when bending an elbow, of jabbing oneself in the eye with the spoon handle? "Well," answered the writer, with barely concealed contempt, "anyone who drinks as hastily as that deserves to hurt himself."

The spoon was so important an element of the drink that, in the book *La Cuisine Creole*, the implement gave the drink its very name. This volume, published in New Orleans in 1885, was written under a pseudonym by the journalist Lafcadio Hearn, who wrote famously about New Orleans and Japan, injecting those exotic worlds into the American imagination. In the book is the requisite recipe for a Whiskey Cocktail (in the "New Orleans Style," which seems to explain the recommended use of Peychaud's bitters, a brand close to the Crescent City's heart since its creation in the early 1800s). But Hearn also suggests "another way" of making the drink. He calls this a "Spoon Cocktail." The formula asks for "one lump of sugar, two dashes Angostura bitters, one piece of lemon peel, one lump of ice. Serve plain in small bar glass with spoon." Well, that's an Old-Fashioned. Though this recipe does not fly under the correct name, an argument could be made that this is

OLD-FASHIONED WHISKEY COCKTAIL.
A photographic demonstration of how this popular drink should be served.

the earliest known printed recipe for the Old-Fashioned, since it is the first to include ice (which is not used in Jerry Thomas's or other early barmen's formulations) and sugar (as opposed to gum syrup).

By the time of Prohibition's repeal, the spoon had largely been forgotten or dispensed with. Why is unclear. Perhaps the new crop of unschooled barmen knew nothing of the old tradition. Or maybe Depression-era bars were economizing and lost spoons could no longer be tolerated. More likely, the use of a spoon was just one of many niceties of barroom behavior that were erased by the Noble Experiment.

Predictably, some traditionalists decried the fact. "Consider, for instance, the old-fashioned cocktail," wrote one "Old Timer" to the *New York Times* on January 1, 1936. "Time was when the affable and sympathetic bartender moistened a lump of sugar with Angostura bitters, dropped in a lump of ice, neither too large nor too small, stuck in a miniature bar spoon and passed the glass to the client with a bottle of good bourbon from which said client was privileged to pour his own drink." Time was, never to return.

CHAPIN, GORE, AND PROULX: THE OLD-FASHIONED HITS THE BOOKS

THE FIRST KNOWN APPEARANCE of the Old-Fashioned, under that name, in a cocktail book came in 1888. The volume is *The Bartender's Manual*. We don't know much about its author, a handsome, dark-eyed, mustachioed young man with the stands-out-in-a-directory name of Theodore Proulx (pronounced "Prue"). What minimal evidence there is suggests that, soon after the book's publication, Proulx left one bar for another—the legal bar—and he may have gotten himself shot in the leg in 1904 by a disgruntled former client.

While we don't know much about Proulx, we do know a lot about the place where he tended bar before collecting his liquid formulas in print. Chapin & Gore was probably the swankiest saloon in Chicago between the end of the Civil War and the turn of the century. It was the haunt of politicians, actors, gamblers, bons vivants, and what the *Chicago Tribune* called, in an 1874 exposé, "fast young men" who lope from the theater box to the bar to discuss the finer "points" of women they knew. Chapin & Gore was the model for Fitzgerald & Moy's, where doomed George Hurstwood worked in Theodore Dreiser's novel *Sister Carrie* before the prosperous, grandly dressed bar manager embezzled funds and stole away with his mistress. (Dreiser based the events in that book partly on his sister Emma's unfortunate affair with a felonious Chapin & Gore cashier.)

Since Old-Fashioned advocate Proulx worked at Chapin & Gore, and an argument can be made that Chicago had a great love for the drink (more on that later), it's worth taking a lingering look at

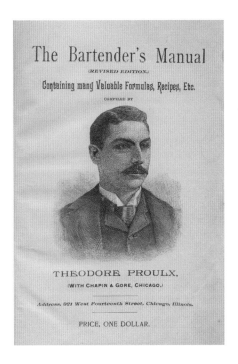

The Bartender's Manual
(REVISED EDITION.)
Containing many Valuable Formulas, Recipes, Etc.
COMPILED BY

THEODORE PROULX,
(WITH CHAPIN & GORE, CHICAGO.)

Address, 921 West Fourteenth Street, Chicago, Illinois.

PRICE, ONE DOLLAR.

this colorful bar and the town that produced it. The first Chapin & Gore bar and restaurant opened in downtown Chicago on Monroe Street, but after a short time there were several branches found around the city. One outlet of typical opulence opened at 47 Clark Street in 1881. It was described as "an exceedingly commodious one, besides being one of the handsomest institutions of its kind in the city," adorned with stained glass, glittering mirrors, chandeliers, cherrywood from floor to ceiling, a cigar stand, and the largest bar mirror in the city.

This bibulous empire was founded by Gardner Spring Chapin and Judge James Jefferson Gore. Gardner, born in 1833 in Whitinsville, Massachusetts, lit out to California to try his luck at mining. There he met another hopeful, Gore. After striking out in California and a more prosaic failure running a dry goods store in Faribault, Minnesota, Chapin opened a grocery with his brother in Chicago in 1865. It was there Gore found him again and convinced him to partner up. They began with a grocery, to which was soon added a liquor department. In 1871, the firm put out its own brand of whiskey, called 1867 Sour Mash (named for the common bourbon distillation process, in which a bit of an older batch of mash is used to spark fermentation in a new batch).

Life was never dull at Chapin & Gore, and sometimes it was violent. In 1880, two gamblers named Howard Barnes and Budd Reno—both on a three-day bender—got into a highly ineffective shootout inside the Monroe Street bar; many bullets flew, neither died, and no arrests were made. Two years earlier, Gore himself was assaulted by two of the notorious Garrity brothers. The Garritys were "local thugs," as the *Tribune* had it, lowlifes whom the paper advised the public to "shoot . . . down like a rabid dog." The ruffians were coercing bar patrons into contributing cash to a fund-raising raffle in support of the family of a third brother, who had been sent up for a train robbery. Gore refused to donate, and the Garritys fell upon him.

A more joyous occasion was May 16, 1873, when Chapin and Gore for the third time purposefully defied a Chicago ordinance requiring bars to close at 11 p.m. Knowing that the police planned to arrest the owners and their bartenders should they flout the law again, a crowd quickly gathered for what promised to be a show to rival anything playing at the nearby McVicker's Theatre.

"The sports were there," recorded a highly amused reporter from the *Tribune*. "The gamblers were there. The fast young men were there. The men who take a pride in going home in the morning stupid with drink were there. Politicians were there. Alderman

Clarke, Tracy and Cullerton were there. All were drinking. Most of them were pretty well 'set up' about that time. They were then 'three sheets in the wind,' to use the national phrase. They were in a state of swearing inebriety. They made it a special point to drink deep and often. That was their method of showing sympathy with the proprietors." On this night, a friendly invitation to drink began with the question "Will you violate?" to which the only proper answer was "Yes, I will violate."

The police finally arrived and arrested the three bartenders— "Piper, Litzen and Geary"—as well as Gore himself and took them to the station house. But Gore had prepared for this. The moment the men left, three bartenders from the Clark Street Chapin & Gore took their places. This sent the crowd into ecstasies. When the replacement trio was arrested (head bartender Mike Boardman "in the spirit of bravado faced the crowd and swallowed a drink"), the original three, who had by then posted bail, resumed their posts. But by then Gore called it quits, rightly concluding that the city had more police than he had bartenders.

It is clear that Chicagoans loved their drink, and the bartending community was robust and respected. Surely Proulx felt his book would find an audience. It seems clear, however, that Proulx's *Bartender's Manual* is not an official Chapin & Gore manual. The tavern was in the habit of publishing a cocktail guide every few years, but most of the subsequent editions were written by longtime bartender Harry W. Stiles, who began working at Chapin & Gore in 1872. These bore the clear-enough title *Chapin & Gore Manual* instead of Proulx's vague parenthetical title-page aside about himself, "With Chapin & Gore of Chicago." In his introduction to the book, moreover, Proulx makes it clear that this is his second effort, a "revised" version of "my first edition," complete with many new drinks "kindly volunteered" by fellow bartenders. He is grateful for "having been so favorably received with my first edition of *Bartender's Manual*." No doubt. This is Proulx's book.

Proulx, during his seemingly short bartending career, was a man of preening confidence. He had advice to impart (much of it quite good) on nearly every aspect of his profession. He made it clear that his volume was a guide to "mixing drinks in the first-class style only" and intended "for bartenders of this class of house only." He also had ambitions. "Every six months, hereafter, I shall issue a circular," he wrote toward the end of the book, "containing the latest drinks since the publication of this book, and a general criticism of bar-tending." Such circulars would be available for the then-princely sum of twenty cents.

There is no evidence that the circulars came to life. So much for Proulx. But to the matter at hand: Proulx offered two methods for making an Old-Fashioned. The first: "Take one-half lump of sugar, and dissolve it with water in a bar or whisky glass, which have the same meaning; then pour out the water; add a little bitters, syrup and absinthe as you would to any other cocktail; twist a piece of lemon-peel; drop in two or three pieces of ice, one jigger of whisky, stir with a spoon and strain into another whisky glass." This recipe, with its absinthe and needlessly complex mix of syrup and sugar, would send Leander Richardson hopping. It reads like an Improved Whiskey Cocktail circa the 1870s.

More on the money is the far simpler method No. 2: "Prepared like the old-fashioned No. 1, with the exception that you use one chunk of ice only and leave it in the glass instead of strain it." The absinthe is still in the thing, but he's getting closer.

THE CHICAGO STYLE

THAT THE OLD-FASHIONED first appeared in a guide written by a bartender associated with Chapin & Gore makes some sense. The firm made a whiskey "as standard as flour," as James Jefferson Gore liked to say, and its clients liked to drink it. One newspaper article referred to the place as a "whiskey market." A Chicago reporter working on a story on popular summer drinks in 1884 stopped inside two different Chapin & Gore taverns to take the barkeeps' pulse. The man behind the Clark Street bar said "there was no particular choice, except the regular whisky straight. A majority of their regular customers took 'the same' summer and winter." At the Monroe branch, meanwhile, many regular customers "took nothing, summer and winter, but plain whisky."

Brawny Chicago had long been a whiskey town. Only three hundred miles from Louisville, it enjoyed a ready supply of Kentucky bourbon. An 1870 survey of the Chicago liquor scene found that, of the $15,600,000 spent every year on booze, fully $9,600,000 of it went to buying whiskey.

Though the prospects of determining the birthplace of the Old-Fashioned are as dim as identifying the first bartender to mix up a Whiskey Cocktail, there's fairly strong evidence that the drink may have begun as a Chicago tipple. In addition to the fact that its first book appearance was in a volume published in Chicago, there are other indicators. An 1899 cocktail book by another bartender with Chicago credentials, John Applegreen, not only had an Old-Fashioned among its cocktails but also contained an entire section dedicated to Old-Fashioned cocktails. (Gin, brandy, and other varieties were included alongside the standard whiskey version.) And it is perhaps worth noting that Leander Richardson, the Midwesterner who blew the whistle on too-fancy Whiskey Cocktails in 1886, put in some years at the *Chicago Inter Ocean* newspaper in the 1870s.

An 1870 *Tribune* survey of the city's drinking scene lists the Whiskey Cocktail (defined as spirit, syrup, lemon, Stoughton's bitters, and, significantly, ice) as a popular local libation. In 1883, the *Tribune* quoted the head bartender at "one of the leading places in the city" as saying, "the old-fashioned cocktails were still in vogue; cocktails made of loaf-sugar and whiskey." Moreover, "they were taken at all hours of the day now, whereas heretofore they were taken as appetizers before breakfast." An 1898 story in the *New York World* told how women at the Waldorf-Astoria Hotel drank on the sly by asking for "tea in the Chicago style," an order that got them a cupful of Whiskey Cocktail.

In 1893, Chicago was the location of the first meeting of the newly formed International Association of Bartenders, an AFL-associated organization made up of sixty-two local unions and eleven thousand members. They convened with the impossible aim of establishing a nationwide standard for making mixed drinks. "Manhattan, Martine, champagne and the old-fashioned cocktails are now mixed in various methods in different cities," read the article.

The Old-Fashioned was considered of such importance that its fate was discussed the very first day. "The old-fashioned cocktail affected by Southern men differs in its composition in various cities," observed one concerned bartender named R. J. McCleary. "It is found in it mellowest, richest state, of course, in the South."

Sol Van Praag, a shady local pol and ward heeler who would later front for Al Capone, was present as an "onlooker and lobbyist," but one with a stated opinion. "Chicagoans drink stronger cocktails than those of other cities," he told the reporter. "I don't want the standard made uniform. When we rejoice here the joy is a deeper, broader quality than that of drinkers of other towns."

As for Gotham, the drink seems to have been slow in arriving. The *New York Sun*, a very wet paper that typically reported on the advancements in the cocktail world with a panting avidity, only got around to printing an account of the "latest drink of the habitués of Madison Square . . . called an 'old-fashioned cocktail,'" in June 1890. "Very soothing and grateful to the palate is this decoction," the *Sun* enthused. "The bartender takes an ordinary cube of loaf sugar and places it gently on the bottom of a thin glass. He sends three dashes of bitters upon the sugar and waits until the sugar has assimilated the bitters and turned the deep crimson color. He then seizes a white cedar pestle—it must be cedar, no other wood will answer—and gently crushes the sugar. A piece of ice as big as a thumbnail is added with a small piece of lemon peel. The drinker then pours his stint of rye whisky into the glass and works the elbow." The amount of ice doesn't jibe with other accounts of the time, and the call for a "thin glass" is curious, since all other recipes ask for a thick-footed vessel, but otherwise the recipe is on the mark. As for the insistence of cedar, drinkers and drink makers have ever had their idiosyncratic certitudes.

THE COLONEL

NONE OF THIS EVIDENCE supporting a Chicago claim to the drink would have moved Colonel Jim Gray, a New Yorker of fabulous bluster and an ego as gaudy the many fantastic waistcoats he owned. Gray presided over the bar at the Fifth Avenue Hotel for nearly thirty years, until it was torn down in April of 1908. At that grand Madison Square political and social center, he served Republican leaders (though he himself was a steadfast Democrat), Civil War generals, and, on one occasion, Chief Joseph of the Nez Perce tribe.

Gray identified himself as the father of the Old-Fashioned.

"Well do I remember the first old fashioned whiskey cocktail made in this house," Colonel Jim told a rapt, if not particularly attentive, reporter from the *New York Sun*. "It was back in 1881. I don't say that other people may not have put up stuff they called old fashioned cocktails, but the first, simple, pure, bona fide drink of that description was compounded by me on the date I have mentioned.

"Really, gentlemen," continued the colonel, who liked to lay it on thick, "I consider it a historic incident not to be compared unfavorably with the Battle of Agincourt, the signing of the Magna Carta or the Fall of Odell. General Grant, to the best of my recollection, was the first to smack his lips over that undiluted nectar of Kentucky corn. I myself, and I say it with pride, invented the formula for the only genuine old fashioned whiskey cocktail."

Gray was convinced that, with the passing of the Fifth Avenue Hotel, one of the grand Madison Square hostelries of beau monde Manhattan, "there won't be a place on earth left where a gentleman can get an old fashioned whiskey cocktail." The problem with his boast, at least as related by the *Sun* article, is that the recipe he shared with the journalist is nothing anyone in the 1910s (or 2010s, for that matter) would recognize as an Old-Fashioned. Gray called for "Loaf sugar, half a lump; Ice, a small cube; Nutmeg, just a sprinkle; Whiskey, two fingers of Fifth Avenue Special; Shake well and for heaven's sake, no bitters."

No bitters? Nutmeg? Shaken?

This formula looked as strange to Gray's contemporaries as it does to us today. And objectors were quick to write to the *Sun* in worried tones. "Nutmeg!" thundered Jabez P. Spine, an agitated Philadelphian, "and to be well shaken!" A Virginia drinker showed the article to Dr. George Williamson, a DC bartending grandee, who replied, "There must be some mistake here. I cannot believe that my esteemed colleague gave this as the recipe for an old fashioned cocktail. He meant it for an old fashioned toddy, and the writer must have confused the two."

Indeed, that does seem to be the likeliest explanation. For there's no doubt that Gray knew how to make an Old-Fashioned and was famous for it (along with his toddy, and a Medford Rum Punch). Other, later newspaper accounts attested to the fact that his way with the drink was beyond reproach. That he invented the drink, though—only Gray himself made that claim.

Like many of the cocktail books published near the end of Prohibition, 1931's *Old Waldorf Bar Days* contained a recipe for the Old-Fashioned. But its author, Albert Stevens Crockett, also tacked on a line of history. He stated that the cocktail was "introduced by, or in honor of, Col. James E. Pepper" and was "the invention of a bartender at the famous Pendennis Club."

That throwaway line has caused a lot of consternation. To this day, the Pendennis Club, a men's club founded in Louisville in 1881, claims to be the birthplace of the drink. It is the only place that makes such a boast.

The club has gone so far as to produce a brief paper on the subject. This 2009 document insists that the drink the club calls its own "was different from the run-of-the-mill 'old fashioned' cocktails then being requested and consumed." The paper lists what it called "several distinctive components," including the exclusive use of Kentucky bourbon instead of other spirits; the use of three fruits (lemon, orange, and cherry), and the fact that those fruits are muddled along with the simple syrup and bitters before ice and the bourbon are added.

If bartenders at the Pendennis were in fact muddling fruit in the 1880s, they were doing so decades before that became common practice in preparing Old-Fashioneds. No known cocktail books published between 1888 (the first appearance of a recipe for the Old-Fashioned) and Prohibition contained such an instruction, and it's a bit far-fetched to believe that the many skilled bartenders who authored those volumes were all getting the Pendennis Club's invention wrong. Not only that, but in the cocktail book published by a former manager at the Pendennis Club, 1914's *Drinks* by the Swiss-born Jacques Straub, the Old-Fashioned is listed, but Straub makes no mention that the drink came from the club that once employed him for two decades, as one might expect he would have.

More confusedly, the club's insistence that muddled fruit is part of the classic recipe clashes directly with its primary source, *Old Waldorf Bar Days*. The recipe in that book makes no mention of fruit whatsoever. If Colonel Pepper gave the recipe used at the Pendennis Club to the Waldorf Hotel, as the book attests, then he gave them the wrong information, at least according to the version described by the Pendennis Club. (Straub's recipe also omits the fruit.)

There are further issues that cast suspicion on the Pendennis Club's authority. *Old Waldorf Bar Days* is presented as a compilation of the drinks made at the Waldorf Hotel, which was built in 1893 at the current site of the Empire State Building. Mentions of the Old-Fashioned Cocktail were common enough in newspapers by that point that Colonel Pepper's recipe would surely have been greeted as old news by the Waldorf's knowledgeable barmen.

Beyond *Old Waldorf Bar Days,* the Pendennis has only the oral accounts of a couple Pendennis bartenders to back up its claim. It is, after all, a private club. There are no minutes, no archives, no printed menus. The organization kept its name out of the papers, so there are no pre-Prohibition news items about the cocktail's link to the club. There is, in fact, no known written mention of the club's connection to the Old-Fashioned until the Waldorf book appeared.

I report all this out of a journalist's sense of due diligence. For at heart, there is really no need for a counterargument to the Pendennis Club's hypothesis that they invented the drink. If the Pendennis Club were laying claim to, say, the Widow's Kiss or the Jack Rose, one might be willing to believe them, for at one moment those drinks didn't exist; and then, suddenly, with the arrival of an ingredient or skilled bartender, they did. The Old-Fashioned is a much more complicated case. Being an outgrowth of the Whiskey Cocktail, it *evolved* more than it *arrived*. Claiming that one bartender created it is a bit like saying a single person invented jazz.

WHAT'S IN A NAME?

NO LAW WAS EVER PASSED declaring the Whiskey Cocktail dead and the Old-Fashioned its rightful successor, of course. And the difference between the two was significant enough that, for a long while, cocktail books contained separate recipes for both drinks. The nomenclature was a bit tortured during this transitional period. Recipes ran under the names "Old-Fashioned Whiskey Cocktail," "Old Fashioned," "Old-Fashioned," "Old Fashion," and "Old-Fashion." People found a dozen ways to name the same damn drink. The same was true at restaurants and bars, with "Whiskey Cocktail" prevailing more often than not on menus until well into the 1910s.

Before a common name could be settled on, the drink, too, began to change. Bartenders being bartenders—that is, inventive, restless, individualistic—some soon seemed to forget the very nature and soul of the drink. Even before the onset of Prohibition, fruit began to appear atop the cocktail as a garnish. Recipes asking for orange bitters as well as Angostura cropped up in the early twentieth century. Curaçao, an orange liqueur once thought banished for good, made a comeback as a suggested accent, as did maraschino liqueur. It was the Gilded Age, after all. Many a swell enjoyed ordering a refreshment as dandified as himself.

Despite these artistic variations, however, the Old-Fashioned soldiered on, gathering popularity over the first two decades of the new century. Henry William Thomas, an esteemed Washington, DC mixologist—whose *Life and Letters* were captured in a biography by author Charles V. Wheeler in 1926—called the drink "this foundation stone of our national independence [which] richly deserved the distinction of its special heavy-bottomed glass." About that glass. Along with the Martini and the Tom Collins, the Old-Fashioned is one of only a few drinks in cocktail history of such august authority that it lent its name to a specific style of glassware. An "Old-Fashioned glass" is a term known to bartenders the world over. It is basically a squat rocks glass, slightly larger than a standard whiskey glass, holding about six to ten ounces and usually tapering slightly at the base. Most importantly, it has a weighted bottom. The purpose of its firm footing was neatly explained by London barman Eddie Clarke in his *Shaking in the '60s*. "The glass must be of sturdy stuff," he stated, "as it has to stand a lot of punishment when the sugar is being pounded up in the mixing of this particular drink."

The style of glass was so well established by the turn of the century that references to the "Old-Fashioned glass" began to pop up in cocktail guides. Early specimens were dainty when compared to what came later. A photo of an Old-Fashioned glass in the *Hoffman House Bartender's Guide* shows a smallish vessel with thin sides but an appropriately stout bottom. When the ponderous double Old-Fashioned glass, holding between twelve and sixteen ounces, made its debut is hard to pinpoint. But following the repeal of Prohibition, during the hard-drinking '40s and '50s, it became the predominant home of the cocktail. Arguably, it became the standard due to its ability to contain all the fruit that was being thrown into the drink during this period.

After Prohibition erased many a bartender's memory of bar practices, some confusedly wondered whether, in fact, the drink had been named after the glass.

REPEAL AND RESURGENCE

PROHIBITION DID NO FAVORS to any cocktail, but it was particularly unkind to the Old-Fashioned. The skilled bartenders who could make a good one either laid down their apron or fled to Europe, Cuba, or other foreign climes to practice their craft. The men who worked speakeasies had neither the time nor the inclination to muck about with muddlers and finely chiseled ice. The drinks being doled out were primitive. Moreover, the Old-Fashioned's chief building block, American whiskey, had been placed in cold storage, the nation's distilleries largely mothballed. (Prohibition, however, was Canadian whisky's chance to shine, as rumrunners funneled vats of the light-bodied stuff across the border to satisfy the thirsty masses, and Americans continued to favor brands such as Canadian Club for decades.)

Still, when Prohibition was finally repealed, the Old-Fashioned—like the Martini, the Manhattan, and a few other drinks too good to completely vanish from American drinkers' dreams—was one of the few classic cocktails that survived the drought. Indeed, it seemed to have gained currency during its long absence. Old-Fashioned glasses (people hadn't forgotten what those were, either), according to one news report, were suddenly in great demand.

"The Old Fashioned cocktail was placed on a pedestal by itself," reported the *New York Times* on November 29, 1933, a week before the 21st Amendment was ratified, while reporting on a Manhattan meeting of the Society of Restaurateurs at Aldine Club at 200 Fifth Avenue. The men were there to talk about liquor prices. Cocktails were expected to be popular. Gin and "bar" whiskey would be priced at thirty cents per drink, "de luxe" drinks like the Clover

Club, Sidecar, Daiquiri, and Jack Rose at thirty-five cents. But the Old-Fashioned, using fully two ounces of whiskey, would run a customer forty cents.

People paid it. "Large hotels throughout the country consulted as to the relative popularity of various cocktails," wrote the *Brooklyn Eagle* in 1935, "report Old Fashioned cocktails leading."

A GOOD OLD-FASHIONED GAL

"THE MOST POPULAR DRINKS in the Times Square and Grand Central districts as well as in the hotels along Park Avenue seemed to be Scotch-and-soda and the 'old-fashioned' cocktail, the base of which is rye whiskey," reported the *New York Times* two days after repeal. "Even more disconcerting to gray-haired waiters with memories of other years was the nonchalance with which women, old and young, ordered their whiskey-and-sodas and gin fizzes. . . . At the Biltmore it was said that the drink most popular with women was the old-fashioned cocktail."

This was a change. Among its many unintentional effects, Prohibition had democratized drinking. Men and women drank side by side in speakeasies. By repeal, the all-male drinking saloon of the pre-Prohibition era was, if not quite dead, at least on its way out. Women had emerged as not just open drinkers but discerning ones, with tastes and criteria that differed from those of their male counterparts.

A *Washington Post* reporter interviewed twenty-five cocktail room captains, liquor store owners, and cafe managers to get to the bottom of the drinking habits of the new demographic. He found women to be curious of mind and stylish in selection. "Women are never ashamed about asking questions about liquor," A. H. German, of Famous Brands, Inc., told the journalist. "They want to know everything there is to know before they make their purchases."

Austin Peterson, manager of Child's Gingham Club, said, "A woman goes down the cocktail list as though the selection of a drink were her life work." M. Quispel, captain of the Willard Hotel Bamboo Room, agreed that ladies liked "artistic drinks," but "love of variety prompts women to sample all the new concoctions offered in the cocktail salons, according to proprietors. But first, they must know the contents. Between sips, they analyze and question. They leave knowing the recipe." After all that sipping and sampling, however, many women settled on the Old-Fashioned. D. G. Lam, manager of the Lotus Club, put the case bluntly: "Women patrons at [my] place order Old Fashioneds more often than any other cocktail. That is because it is sweet and flavorful. Women are partial to sweet, light, aromatic drinks. They prefer mixtures to straight liquor." Sometimes these preferences took them in a direction far away from the cocktail's technical definition. In 1934, the New Yorker reported, "Lots of places are getting accustomed to having ladies ask for . . . Old-Fashioneds made with just whiskey and fruit—no sugar or bitters."

In one installment of "Her Heart to a Stranger," a newspaper serial by Peter B. Kyne, an ornery old westerner puts his son's citified fiancée to the test, telling her to fix him an "old-fashioned bourbon whiskey cocktail." "This dude girl will use rye instead o' bourbon an' jazz it up with a cherry, a slice of orange, a hunk o' pineapple, an' charged water—New York style," he remarks. But the girl is his match. "I'm a dude," she says, "but I know the difference between an old-fashioned and a fruit salad."

It is perhaps significant that two popular songs of the era named after the drink were sung by women. "A Good Old-Fashioned Cocktail (with a Good Old-Fashioned Gal)," written by Harry Warren and Al Dubin, was first delivered by Ruby Keeler in the 1935 film Go into Your Dance, in which she starred with then-husband Al Jolson. The lyric went:

Modern living is surely giving us too much speed to last,
We eat and drink and live too fast.
You'll discover that I'm a lover of good old-fashioned ways,
Let's harken back to bygone days.
If you're feeling kind of lonely and you feel you need a pal,
Have a good Old-Fashioned cocktail with a good old-
fashioned gal.
While you tell her of your travels 'round the Panama Canal,
Have a good Old-Fashioned cocktail with a good old-
fashioned gal.
And tho' it's great and up to date to liquidate your liquor
straight,
It's more sedate to get "Hey Hey" the good old-fashioned way.
You can cry upon her shoulder, sing about your old gal Sal;
Have a good Old-Fashioned cocktail with a good old-
fashioned gal.

By 1940, Cole Porter was content to have Hattie Maloney, the nightclub-owning heroine in *Panama Hattie*, played by Ethel Merman, drown her sorrows in Old-Fashioneds. Went the chorus:

Waiter, make it another Old-Fashioned, please
Make it another, double, Old-Fashioned, please
Make it for one who's due to join the disillusion crew
Make it for one of love's new refugees.

THE FRUIT WARS

AS EVER, THIS SURGE in the Old-Fashioned's popularity among a new demographic of drinkers rubbed certain people—particularly ancient tipplers who could remember the before-times—the wrong way. By their account, there had been a falling off in quality. As cultural critic Gilbert Seldes put it, "Prohibition has created a nation of men and women who do not know what to do with the liquor they so hardly come by."

"Consider, for instance, the old-fashioned cocktail," began an ominous 1936 letter to the editor at the *New York Times*. (The author of the letter was the same "Old Timer" who remembered the days of the Old-Fashioned spoon.) "Nowadays the modern or ex-speakeasy bartender drops a spoonful of powdered sugar into a glass, adds a squirt of carbonic to aid dissolution, adds to that a dash or two of some kind of alleged bitters and a lump of ice, regardless of size. Then he proceeds to build up a fruit compote of orange, lemon, pineapple and cherry, and himself pours in a carefully measured ounce and a half of bar whiskey, usually a blend, and gives one a glass rod to stir it with. Price, 35 to 50 cents. Profanation and extortion."

"There are a few old-time bartenders working now and they commit these crimes with tears in their eyes," the old-timer continued. "But they say the present generation of drinkers wants them that way, that the present customs were adopted during prohibition to disguise the horrible taste of the terrible liquor. . . . Prohibition has much to answer for besides crime and racketeering."

And so the fruit wars began: a battle between purity and frippery, between paring the drink down and loading it up. The struggle continues to this very day. Fruit had made plenty of appearances in Old-Fashioneds prior to Prohibition. But it was almost always used as a decorative garnish, and even back then, there were folks who complained of it. Humorist Don Marquis—the *New York Sun* columnist who created the deathless cockroach and cat, Archy and Mehitabel—published a series of pre-Prohibition sketches featuring the ruminations of a character called the Old Soak. In one, he calls for an Old-Fashioned Whiskey Cocktail with not "too much orange and that kind of damned garbage" in it. "I want the kick."

Old Soak and his friends would have had no difficulty finding a bartender sympathetic to the idea of a fruit-free Old-Fashioned back in the days before the Volstead Act. After Prohibition, however, fruit seemed to be the rule. And the produce was everywhere: on top of the drink as an orange-cherry "flag"; swimming at the bottom of the drink; and, horror of horrors, muddled along with the sugar and bitters prior to the addition of whiskey, producing a sort of Old-Fashioned soup. This was the case not only in the United States but also in London, Paris, Spain, and elsewhere. During an era when the Martini grew progressively stronger—with the gin to vermouth ratio growing apart at a staggering rate, to the point where vermouth nearly disappeared completely—the Old-Fashioned grew weaker and wan.

Some people liked it this way—many, in fact, or the style wouldn't have persisted. How did this all happen? It could be, as "Old Timer" pointed out, that fruit was used more generously during Prohibition to disguise the poor quality of the liquor. Cocktail historian David Wondrich thinks the drink might have become confused with another cocktail, the fruitier toddy, and the divide between the two tipples collapsed.

Harry Craddock perhaps deserves some of the blame/credit here. His *Savoy Cocktail Book*, published in the 1930s, was a vital guide for many bartenders returning to—or first coming to—their work. And Craddock's Old-Fashioned recipe says to decorate with twist of lemon peel and a slice of orange.

The owners of Sloppy Joe's in Havana, too, may bear some responsibility for the fruitification of the drink. Cuba was a favorite retreat of parched Americans during Prohibition. Here they discovered the joys of rum, the Daiquiri, and bars like La Floridita and Sloppy Joe's. The latter bar put out an annual book of recipes for many years, and its "Old Fashion" formula was about as fruity as they come. In the bar's 1932–33 edition—published just as Prohibition was ending—the drink asks for curaçao, slices of lemon, pineapple, and orange, and a cherry. (A 1937 recipe from the same series also called for a slice of lime. Only in the tropics!) It's impossible that a few Americans didn't return to their newly wet homeland with this version fresh in their memory. Meanwhile, the famous Oscar of the Waldorf—that is, Oscar Tschirky, the longtime majordomo of that high-end hotel—insisted in 1935 that an Old-Fashioned be made with orange, cherry, and pineapple.

Craddock and Sloppy Joe's stopped short of advising smashing up the fruit. Muddling didn't become common until the 1970s, although it was practiced as early as the 1930s. *Burke's Complete Cocktail & Drinking Recipes*, a widely distributed volume from 1934 by Harman Burney Burke, told the Old-Fashioned builder to "add one Slice of Orange, one Slice of Lemon Peel, mull [meaning muddle] with the Bitters and Sugar, then add the Whiskey and serve in the same glass." That this recipe appeared the year after repeal lends some credence to the theory of the "Old Timer" that muddled fruit was used to mask the flavor of bad booze during Prohibition.

Some, however, have argued that the cocktail's descent into sweetness began before the nation officially dried up. One "Metcalfe," a hilarious malcontent, pontificated in the *Wall Street*

Journal in 1925 that "modern effeminacy and degeneration had destroyed an old American institution and robbed Volstead and his law of some of their sting." Vermouth was an early villain in Metcalfe's story. The Manhattan and Martini were "still a he-drink," in his opinion, "but degeneration started with the addition of maraschino cherries, olives and other foreign substances for the sake of looks more than flavor." Metcalfe continued, "Some vandal then invented the Bronx cocktail which, through omission of the distinguished bitters, had no right to the generic name. From that to the Orange Flower cocktail, which derives its title from the addition of a flavoring extract, the descent was easy. It would be impossible to enumerate the other mixtures, sweetened, lemon-juiced, fruited, spiced and flavored, which destroyed appetite instead of stimulating it, and desecrated the name of cocktail."

However the alternative style came about, the fruit-salad style sent Old-Fashioned purists into conniptions as nothing had since the dark days of the 1870s, when mixologists tried to dash curaçao and absinthe into Whiskey Cocktails. Reactionary conservative columnist Westbrook Pegler, never one to mince words, called the Old-Fashioned, circa 1938, "A fruit salad dunked in rye and crowned with a sprig of turnip greens." Journalist and wit Lucius Beebe, in his introduction to Crosby Gaige's *Cocktail Guide and Ladies' Companion* of 1945, told a tale (doubtless amply embroidered) of an encounter with the barman at Chicago's Drake Hotel. He asked for an Old-Fashioned but cautioned "without fruit except the lemon":

> *The Nestor of the decanters waxed as livid as a Marxist on May Day, smashed a champagne glass he was polishing and danced up and down on the duck-boards in an ecstasy*

of rage. "Young impudent sir," he screamed, "my hair is hoary—witheld," he added as an afterthought. "Man and boy I've built Old Fashioned cocktails these sixty years. Yes sir, since the first Armour was pushing a wheelbarrow in a slaughterhouse, and I have never yet had the perverted nastiness of mind to put fruit in an Old Fashioned. Get out, scram, go over to the Palmer House and drink."

Alas, there were far fewer bartenders of the Drake standard than there were new recruits who did what the flood of new post-Prohibition cocktail guides told them to without question. And most of these volumes called unfailingly for orange, cherry, and often pineapple. Moreover, they advised a squirt of seltzer. The soon-to-be-ubiquitous *Mr. Boston* manuals, named for a Beantown distillery, were first introduced in 1935. Its Old-Fashioned recipe called for lemon, orange, and cherry, a formula that went largely unchanged for decades. Ditto the *Cocktail and Wine Digest*, published every year from 1943 into the 1970s by a man who became president of the International Bar Managers' Association. No less a guide than *Esquire's Handbook for Hosts*, published in 1949, advised that produce "may be added" (even canned pineapple was okay), but the periodical knew it was kicking a hornet's nest in just suggesting such a thing.

"Them what likes their Old-Fashioneds without sugar, without bitters, without water or seltzer, without ice and certainly without fruit are just too old-fashioned to name their drink as 'straight whiskey, please,'" winked the *Esquire* editors. "Actually, the only debatable part of an Old-Fashioned is the fruit garnish—the cherry, orange-slice and sometime stick of pineapple which serious drinkers claim interfere with their Old-Fashioned elbow-bending."

(*Continues on page 56*)

The Old-Fashioned didn't completely die during the final years of the twentieth century. Certain pockets of the United States served as refuges. One was Wisconsin, a state not quickly swayed by fashion. Here the Old-Fashioned never went out of style and could safely be ordered at any bar, from a swanky supper club to a county tap. It was as close to an official state drink as the Badger State had.

There was a twist, however, to ordering an Old-Fashioned in Wisconsin. Unless you specified otherwise, it was made with brandy.

Wisconsin loves its brandy. For many years, the state consumed more of the spirit than anyone else in the United States. Not surprisingly for a populace better known for its beer intake, the favorite brand is light-bodied California-made Korbel. Of the 323,000 cases of brandy produced by the California-based winery and distillery in 2012, some 140,000 went to the Badger State.

The ritual surrounding the Brandy Old-Fashioned in Wisconsin goes beyond an insistence on Korbel. Each cocktail begins in roughly the same way: with an orange slice and a cherry muddled in a rocks glass with sugar and Angostura bitters, followed by the brandy and then ice. A call for "sweet" means it's topped off with 7-Up or Sprite; "sour" gets you sour mix or a tarter soda brand, like Squirt. And "press" is finished with a combination of 7-Up and soda water. Some patrons (usually older ones) request their drinks be finished with pickled mushrooms, onions, or brussels sprouts.

Why Wisconsin laps up so many barrels of brandy has long been a subject of speculation. The most plausible theory was laid out in a 2006 article in the Madison paper, the *Isthmus*. The paper pointed out that the wine-making Korbel brothers exhibited their new brandy at the 1893 World's Columbian Exposition in Chicago, which attracted twenty-seven million visitors, many of them from neighboring Wisconsin. (Not surprisingly, nearby Minnesota also likes brandy, and Illinois and Michigan are no slouches either.) Also, the Germans and Scandinavians who settled in the Midwest brought a taste for brandy with them from the Old Country.

The state's thirst for the Brandy Old-Fashioned has not slackened since the exposition. The ritual of the Friday-night fish fry, slavishly followed for decades, traditionally begins with an Old-Fashioned. (Brandy Manhattans are also a common sight.) Even virgin drinkers know this. In the winter of 1967, a group of students at the University of Wisconsin–Whitewater pranked it up at the Ice-O-Rama by sculpting a giant Old-Fashioned out of ice blocks, right down to a giant orange slice.

The drink has become such a local institution that when, in 2005, Jennifer DeBolt and her partners decided to open a bar and restaurant in Madison, a stone's throw from the state capitol, they named it The Old-Fashioned. The place can sell 2,500 a week and goes through ten cases of Korbel during that same time span.

David Embury, a lawyer who in 1958 published *The Fine Art of Mixing Drinks*, one of the most comprehensive of the postwar cocktail guides, tried to set the record straight. But, in lawyerly fashion, he ended up splitting too many hairs in making his case. He bravely stated, "Water, either plain or charged, has no more place in an Old Fashioned than it has in a Manhattan or a Martini." Hear, hear! Welcome frankness. But then he muddied the waters by offering an alternate recipe, a fruit-laden "Old Fashioned De Luxe" (an oxymoron of a name if there ever was one). "My own opinion is that fruit flavors and liquors blend exquisitely and that, for a mid-afternoon or an evening drink, an Old Fashioned is greatly improved in its over-all appeal by the judicious addition of a few fruits." He even went so far as to recommend, "for a change," pouring in some juice from the maraschino cherry bottle, or a dash of curaçao, Cointreau, the herbal French liqueur green Chartreuse, or Strega, the saffron-tinted liqueur from Campania, Italy. It's enough to send a purist to his sickbed.

POSTWAR HEYDAY

FRUITED OR NOT, the Old-Fashioned experienced one its great heydays in the two decades or so following the end of Prohibition. By 1940, the *New Yorker* was calling it a "national institution." It was one of only five cocktails featured at the popular Child's chain of restaurants, which boasted that its every bartender was "a master of his craft." It was on all hotel bar menus, every bill of fare in every train's dining car. Chinese restaurants and Jewish delis offered them. The drink was so popular that, recalled 1950s New York barman Brian Rea, bartenders used to prepare a "bug juice" mixture of Angostura bitters and simple syrup in order to eliminate a step and meet demand more quickly. Another time-saver was sugar cubes presoaked in bitters. Drinkers still took pains to specify their style of Old-Fashioned: with lemon peel only; with fruit as garnish; with muddled fruit; with soda or no soda. But they drank them by the gallon.

There were shortcuts for home use as well. In 1941, a time-saving gimmick arrived in the form of a box of twenty-eight "beautiful, rosy-red" cubes that combined "the acrid aspect of the cocktail with the essential sugar," thus eliminating the need to judge exactly what a "dash" of bitters was. The set came complete with a small muddler.

By the late 1950s and early '60s, however, the Old-Fashioned—and whiskey drinks in general—went into eclipse. The Smirnoff "Leaves You Breathless" ad campaign had been phenomenally successful, and vodka was in the ascendant. Three-Martini lunches became vodka affairs, with the traditional gin increasingly taking a backseat. The 1970s and '80s were no better. Foolishly simple club drinks, with equally foolish names (Harvey Wallbanger, Sex on the Beach, Fuzzy Navel) dominated youthful drinking. Discos were no place for the contemplative consumption an Old-Fashioned fosters. Those who continued to favor the cocktail drank them at home, where they could expect a well-built drink. By the final decades of the twentieth century, a young bartender was easily stumped by a request for an Old-Fashioned, and the patron ordering the drink was quickly tagged as a hopeless old fogey.

A couple places kept the drink's reputation alive. One haven was the American Midwest (see page 54). Another was London. The UK never adopted the fruited style favored by Yankees. But their version came with its own quirks.

In the 1990s and early 2000s, a customer who ordered an Old-Fashioned in London needed patience. As the city's bartenders made it, the drink was built incrementally. Bitters and sugar were put in the glass, plus one third of the bourbon and ice. The mixture was then stirred. Then the second third of the bourbon and ice was introduced. More stirring. Finally, the last of the whiskey and ice joined the mix. Further stirring. Several minutes later, some poor sap had his drink.

This painstakingly diluted version can be traced back to Dick Bradsell, godfather of London's modern mixology scene and a devotee of David Embury's iconic 1948 cocktail book, *The Fine Art of Mixing Drinks*. Embury indicated that the Old-Fashioned, as originally made, took a full twenty minutes to construct.

Because of the free exchange of citizenry between the UK and Australia, this method became common Down Under as well. But, with the global spread of information among the bartender community, it began to die out by the 2010s. Just as well. As barman Dale DeGroff said, "I'd much rather have the dilution occur while I'm drinking it, not at the bar. I want it to get better on my watch, not yours."

Mad Men, the AMC television series set in a Madison Avenue advertising agency during the smoking, drinking, and womanizing New York of the early 1960s, may not have ushered in the revival of the Old-Fashioned, but it certainly didn't hinder its progress. The drink is the poison of choice of Don Draper, the show's enigmatic, charismatic antihero. In season one, episode one, which aired on July 17, 2007, before we know Draper's name or occupation, we learn his drink preference. "Do this again," he tells a waiter. "Old-Fashioned, please." Soon after, *Mad Men*–themed cocktail parties were being thrown, and many an Old-Fashioned was thrown back.

The Old-Fashioneds that Draper drinks are specific to the period. They're watery, filled with cheap ice, and adorned with an orange slice and cherry. He prefers Canadian Club, a whisky that flourished during Prohibition (even in the 1960s, the north-of-the-border whisky was still regarded as the good stuff).

While Draper isn't particular about liquor brand or the method of preparation when ordering an Old-Fashioned in a bar or restaurant, his at-home preferences are made clear in season three in an episode in which he is shown making his drink step by step. His execution isn't the daintiest. He first sets up a couple of Old-Fashioned glasses and plunks a sugar cube and a cherry in both. Each cube is doused with Angostura bitters. He reaches for Old Overholt rye (he's at a Kentucky Derby party at a country club, and there's no bourbon behind the bar). A glassful of ice is scooped up. Into this glass, he free pours a good measure of rye and a near equal amount of club soda. He then returns to the glasses and muddles the sugar and cherries. The glass of whiskey and water is given a cursory mix with a bar spoon, and then poured—ice and all—directly into the waiting cocktail glasses. Finally, an orange slice is popped into each glass.

It's very likely that the pick-up artist played by Ryan Gosling in the 2011 comedy *Crazy, Stupid, Love* had Don Draper in mind as he prepared a couple of Old-Fashioneds for himself and his latest conquest, portrayed by Emma Stone. However, he doesn't make the drink like Draper; he builds it as well as any modern bar artist, exhibiting a minimalist approach and slicing off a swath of orange peel the size of a bookmark. Perhaps, in his character, *Mad Men* and mixology meet.

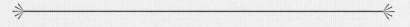

REBIRTH AND CULT STATUS

THE DISMAL FATE of the long-suffering cocktail was largely reversed by a former actor named Dale DeGroff. In 1987, restaurateur Joe Baum made DeGroff the head bartender at the Rainbow Room. Baum tossed DeGroff an old copy of Jerry Thomas's nineteenth-century cocktail manual and instructed him to create a menu of classic cocktails. After decades spent in the deep freeze, drinks like the Bronx, Ramos Gin Fizz, Sazerac, and Stork Club Cocktail made a reappearance, confusing young drinkers and jarring old ones with a shock of happy recognition. Old-Fashioneds, too, were served, and ordered in abundance.

"Anyone who grew up in the '50s and was missing the idea that they could get a great Daiquiri or great Whiskey Sour—it had been years," said DeGroff. "Everything tasted like that awful sour mix. When the word got out that we were doing these drinks, and it didn't take long, we were slammed. The Old-Fashioned sold like hotcakes."

DeGroff insisted on many of the practices that are now common behind the best cocktail bars: using freshly squeezed juice, quality liquor, and large ice cubes and seeking out hard-to-get ingredients, which were needed to correctly make old recipes. His Old-Fashioned, however, was not that of the 1880s. It was the postwar, muddled, fruited rendition, a style that DeGroff had grown up with and defends to this day as "punchy and wonderful tasting."

It was that version that he passed on to the new generation of young epicurean bartenders who looked upon him as a rare mentor in what had become a devalued profession.

While everyone admired DeGroff, not everyone agreed with him. As early as 2002, *Esquire* cocktail columnist David Wondrich was punching back, calling the "properly made," no-fruit Old-Fashioned one of the four essential drinks every serious-minded drinker should know—the others being the Martini, Manhattan, and Daiquiri. When Wondrich designed the cocktail menu for a Brooklyn bar called Chickenbone in early 2003, he put the "garbage"-free Old-Fashioned at the top of the list. In those early years of the new millennium, the debate over the cocktail raged fiercely among the small, clannish group that cared about such things. The chatroom of *DrinkBoy*, a cultish, influential website created by Robert Hess, was a frequent forum of these disputations. Discussions about the history and true nature of the Old-Fashioned began to appear on the site in the late 1990s, with Hess, Wondrich, and other regulars typically arguing in favor of the fruit-free version. "Properly made the Old Fashioned is a simply wonderful drink, and it is the first drink I always request of any new bartender," wrote Hess in one post in 2000. "While 9 times out of 10 they don't do it right, how 'wrong' they do it helps me to judge their knowledge, skill, and appreciation for truly understanding the art of bartending."

With time, Hess & Co. had their way in the best barrooms. When Dushan Zaric and his partners opened up the speakeasy-style cocktail lounge Employees Only in Greenwich Village in 2004, they offered the fruited Old-Fashioned that DeGroff had taught them. Later, as tastes changed in the backward-looking cocktail community, they switched to an older Old-Fashioned, sans fruit. When DeGroff's disciple, Audrey Saunders, opened the Pegu Club in SoHo in 2005, fruit was included only if a patron insisted. Otherwise, it was a lemon twist with a rye Old-Fashioned, an orange twist with a Bourbon Old-Fashioned. A similar version was served at the influential San Francisco speakeasy Bourbon & Branch when it opened its secret door in 2006.

The era of retro austerity had begun. By the end of the first decade of the current century, the vast majority of the country's best mixologists recoiled at the very suggestion of fruit in an Old-Fashioned. A bit of water to dissolve a bit of sugar, a dash or two of Angostura bitters, one large ice cube, and two ounces of fine rye or bourbon—*that* was an Old-Fashioned. The drink became the test by which bartenders measured the skills and attitudes of their colleagues. Having it on the menu was like having a Model T in your garage. In short time, cocktail enthusiasts, too, became equally uncompromising in their definition of an Old-Fashioned.

While the bar artists of the 2000s celebrated the Old-Fashioned's return to its origins, they also recognized the recipe as a piece of sturdy architecture on which to hang alternative interpretations of the classic. There was scarcely a name mixologist who didn't have an Old-Fashioned variation or two up his or her sleeve. And so the Oaxaca Old-Fashioned of Phil Ward, an agave enthusiast, quickly gathered steam as a modern classic, as did the fat-washed, bacon-flavored Benton's Old-Fashioned of Don Lee. As new spirits appeared on the market, twists using unaged white whiskey, absinthe, and elderflower liqueur popped up. At the San Francisco bar Hog & Rocks, bartender Michael Lazar collected a selection of these variations on a separate mini-cocktail menu he called "Pimp My Old-Fashioned."

The base spirit was only one entryway into reinterpreting the drink's formula. Bitters production exploded in the twenty-first century. Angostura was no longer your only option. In addition to the dozens of new products on the market, bartenders also created their own. The difference between a standard Old-Fashioned and a Prime Meats Old-Fashioned, served at the Brooklyn eatery Prime Meats, lies in the pear bitters made in house by barman Damon Boelte.

The choice of sweetener to harmonize with the cocktail's other ingredients became another way in which mixologists could vary the drink. The blanket application of simple syrup was, well, simple-minded. Mixing with tequila or mezcal? Use agave syrup. Funky rums called for molasses, and some meatier whiskeys were better complemented by maple syrup. Honey syrups, ginger syrups, and a host of liqueurs served similar purposes.

Through their simultaneous embrace of retro purity and forward-looking creativity, mixologists created a bit of a headache for themselves by asking patrons to hold two contradictory ideas inside their heads. While with one hand they were self-righteously keeping adulterating agents such as muddled fruit and Sprite at bay, with the other they were finding their own ways to "improve" the supposedly unimprovable Old-Fashioned. They must also bear the blame for creating the modern Old-Fashioned snob, the sort of drinker whose back gets up if he sees a cherry within one hundred feet of a rye bottle.

Same as it ever was. Life will never be completely calm on those bright amber waters. Until that first soothing sip, of course.

In 1996, William Grimes, the author of the prescient 1993 book *Straight Up or On the Rocks*, wrote, comparing various drinks to the Martini, "The daiquiri, the old-fashioned and the Manhattan all rank as classics. None of them have inspired a cult." Today, thanks to the mixologists mentioned here and the drinkers who take their instruction, this is no longer true. The Old-Fashioned has a sizable following of worshipful adherents, among whom the debate never ends.

And it is worth fighting over. For, to its faithful, it contains things that merit defending. Within its 1806 embodiment of the cocktail incarnate—spirit, sweetener, bitters, water—there is traditionalism. Amid the many variations that have followed, there is liberty and invention. By sticking to the variation you hold by, there is individualism. Moreover, it's democratic: anyone can make one. No wonder Americans like the drink. There's a lot of America in it.

THE RECIPES

HERE ARE A FEW GUIDELINES on the basics of preparing Old-Fashioneds, with tips on the requisite equipment and ingredients you will need.

EQUIPMENT

To prepare the recipes in this book, you will need a few pieces of equipment, all easily attainable at any kitchenware store. They include:

⇒ **AN OLD-FASHIONED GLASS (6 TO 10 OUNCES)**

⇒ **A DOUBLE OLD-FASHIONED GLASS (12 TO 16 OUNCES)** For those recipes more laden with fruit and other "improvements," a larger glass is merited.

⇒ **A STANDARD MIXING GLASS** Many Old-Fashioned recipes are built and served inside the same glass. However, a few included here are prepared in a mixing glass. A pint glass can be used in a pinch. I prefer mixing glasses to cocktail tins, for the simple reason that you can see inside a glass and keep track of how much you are diluting your drink. Many barware companies sell beautiful Japanese-style cut mixing glasses, which come in glass and crystal. Naturally, these are more expensive than your standard pint glass; however, they are a beautiful addition to any home bar.

⇒ **A BARSPOON** A long (approximately 11-inch) barspoon is the preferred tool for stirring drinks.

⇒ **A JIGGER** Most jiggers are stainless steel and have a dual-measure design. Modern Mixologist makes a very versatile double jigger: one end has a 1½-ounce capacity; the other has a 1-ounce capacity.

⇴ **A JULEP COCKTAIL STRAINER AND/OR A HAWTHORNE COCKTAIL STRAINER** Only a few of the drinks here require straining; use a julep strainer for drink made solely of spirits, a Hawthorne strainer in the few drinks where fresh juice is involved.

⇴ **A MUDDLER** In the earliest days of the American cocktail, muddlers were made of wood. Today, there are rubber and steel variants. I still find that the old-fashioned wooden model works best.

If you want to get particular, and don't mind spending a little extra, I strongly recommend the bar equipment put out by Cocktail Kingdom (www.cocktailkingdom.com) and Modern Mixologist (www.themodernmixologist.com). For muddlers, there's none better than the hand-crafted Pug Muddlers made in New York State (www.wnjones.com/pug). They cost a bit, but you'll never need another. If you want to have a little fun shopping, antique and vintage shops are good sources for Old-Fashioned glasses of various designs and styles.

INGREDIENTS

The cocktail renaissance has spurred an increase in the production and availability of quality spirits, liqueurs, and bitters. Most cities now contain at least one or two well-curated liquor shops that can satisfy a home mixologist's every spirituous need. (Or, at the very least, they can order the desired ingredient.) If you don't have access to a specialty liquor shop, you can order many of the goods you need online: The Boston Shaker (www.thebostonshaker.com) and The Meadow (www.atthemeadow.com) have an excellent selection of bitters, while caskstore.com and astorwines.com have a nice array of specialty spirits and liqueurs.

ICE

I cannot emphasize enough the importance of using large blocks of ice in most Old-Fashioned recipes. Apart from avoiding the rapid dilution of your cocktail, anchoring your cocktail with a single chunk of well-shaped frozen water will greatly increase the cocktail's aesthetic appeal. The cubes created using standard ice trays will not do. Several companies, including Cocktail Kingdom (www.cocktailkingdom.com), the Boston Shaker (www.theboston shaker.com), and even some housewares stores, sell specialized trays that created large-form cubes. A neat trick that will cost you no more than fifty cents is to fill and freeze water balloons, resulting in lovely ice spheres.

Finally, if ice has been sitting in your freezer for more than a week, do not use it in drinks. Throw it out and make a fresh batch. Old ice will absorb other flavors lurking in your freezer.

SWEETENERS

If you prefer to use simple syrup (see box on page 73) where sugar is called for, go ahead. Just keep in mind that ¼ ounce is the rough equivalent to one sugar cube. But, since the ritual of muddling a sugar cube is so much part and parcel of the Old-Fashioned's history, I recommend that route with most of these recipes (the exception being some of the modern iterations featured later in the book, which call for specific syrups and infusions). Make sure to use a barspoon of warm water, the better to dissolve the sugar. However, if some sugar remains at the bottom of the glass, don't fret. It didn't bother your ancestors. And that's what the Old-Fashioned spoon is for. Scoop it up. It's dessert.

Many of the drinks that follow call for syrup instead of lump sugar. At its most basic, cocktail syrup is either "simple" or "rich." Below are recipes for each.

SIMPLE SYRUP

MAKES 1 CUP

1 cup sugar

1 cup water

Heat the sugar and water in a saucepan over medium heat, stirring occasionally until the sugar has dissolved. The moment the water begins to boil, remove from the heat, let cool, then refrigerate. Stored tightly sealed in the refrigerator, the syrup will keep for 1 week.

DEMERARA SYRUP (AKA RICH SYRUP)

MAKES ½ CUP

1 cup Demerara sugar

½ cup water

Heat the sugar and water in a saucepan over medium heat, stirring occasionally until the sugar has dissolved. The moment the water begins to boil, remove from the heat, let cool, then refrigerate. Stored tightly sealed in the refrigerator, the syrup will keep for 1 week.

BITTERS

A dash is whatever comes out of a bottle of bitters when you upend it with a swift flick of the wrist. In the past few years, the market has become flooded with literally hundreds of new brands of bitters. But even the most enthusiastic home bartender need only have a dozen or so. Angostura is, of course, the essential item, particularly where the Old-Fashioned is concerned. Peychaud's, called for in a few of the recipes that follow, should be your second purchase. Among the many orange bitters now available, I prefer Angostura's version as the most well-rounded and complex. Other versatile bitters I like and have found work in an Old-Fashioned include:

- Fee Brothers whiskey barrel–aged bitters
- The Bitter Truth aromatic bitters
- Dutch's colonial bitters

GARNISHES

If you don't have fresh citrus on hand to provide the drink's garnish, don't make the drink. Just as much as the bitters, the twist is part of the recipe and completes the overall flavor. For the recipes in the Standard Variations section (page 86), I recommend a twist at least 2 inches long and ¾ inch wide. Of course, if you prefer your twist smaller or larger, please suit yourself. To remove the twist, use either a peeler or a knife, and try to cut away just the skin, leaving behind as much of the bitter white pith as possible. Twist the garnish over the drink and rub it along the edges of the glass to release the citrus oils, then slip it into the drink, nestling the twist along the side between the glass and the ice cube.

STIRRING

"Stir until chilled" usually means stirring for about 30 seconds.

OLD SCHOOL

An Old-Fashioned drinker is a drinker who is curious about history. With that in mind, collected here are a few formulas of historical interest, for those nights when you feel like drinking as your forebears did. Except where indicated, the recipes are given as originally printed in the cocktail books in which they appeared.

WHISKEY COCKTAIL

JERRY THOMAS, *HOW TO MIX DRINKS, OR
THE BON VIVANT'S COMPANION,* **1862**

W here better to begin the recipe portion of this book than with this, the Old-Fashioned's direct ancestor? The recipe that follows comes from the book *How to Mix Drinks, or the Bon Vivant's Companion* by Jerry Thomas, a celebrated mixologist of his day who etched a place in cocktail history by authoring the first cocktail recipe book ever printed. You'll note that this ur-recipe differs from the contemporary Old-Fashioned in several ways: no ice, syrup instead of sugar, and a stemmed glass instead of the traditional Old-Fashioned or rocks glass. In Thomas's time, the whiskey used would likely have been rye, which was historically popular in the eastern states. He calls for a "wine-glass" measure of whiskey, the equivalent of 2 ounces. For the Boker's, a popular bitters at the time of the book's publication, you can substitute Angostura or another aromatic bitters of similar character, if you please. A half barspoon of simple syrup (page 73) will equal the dashes of gum syrup prescribed. (If you want to stick with gum syrup, it can be bought from companies such as Small Hands Foods.) You may want to go sweeter, but there's something nice about the austerity of this drink's drier form. Cracked ice will do for the "fine" ice called for here. There were no "Old-Fashioned glasses" back then, so if you want a period-correct drink, use a small, squat wineglass—it should have about a 6-ounce capacity. The 1887 edition of Thomas's book listed an Improved Whiskey Cocktail that called for dashes of absinthe and maraschino liqueur.

3 or 4 dashes of gum syrup
2 do. bitters (Boker's)
1 wine-glass of whiskey, and a piece of lemon peel.

Fill one-third full of fine ice; shake and strain in a fancy red wine-glass.

Col. Jim Gray's

OLD-FASHIONED WHISKEY COCKTAIL

NEW YORK SUN, 1908

"Colonel" Jim Gray enjoyed a thirty-year tenure behind the bar at New York's Fifth Avenue Hotel. He contended that he had served the Old-Fashioned Whiskey Cocktail since 1881 and had, in fact, invented it. This is the recipe given to a *New York Sun* reporter in 1908 by Colonel Gray himself. This formula is patently *not* an Old-Fashioned, what with the lack of bitters and lemon peel and the presence of nutmeg. Most likely, the reporter mistakenly applied the name to the recipe for a Whiskey Toddy, another drink for which Gray was famous. Indeed, several bartenders wrote to the *Sun* protesting that Gray must have been misquoted. Nonetheless, this is the recipe we have. And, taken as such, it's actually an excellent drink. The recipe below is adapted from Gray's instructions to the *Sun*.

2 ounces bourbon or rye

1 sugar cube

Dash of nutmeg

Muddle the sugar cube, a barspoon of water, and a sprinkle of nutmeg in a mixing glass. Add the whiskey and ice. Attach tin to top of glass and shake the drink. Strain the drink into an Old-Fashioned glass. Dust with nutmeg. "And, for heavens sake," as the Colonel said, "no bitters."

Methods No. 1 & 2

OLD-FASHIONED COCKTAIL

THEODORE PROULX, ADAPTED FROM
THE BARTENDER'S MANUAL, **1888**

Theodore Proulx, a onetime bartender at the grand Chicago saloon Chapin & Gore, is the author of another early cocktail book, this one called *The Bartender's Manual,* published in 1888. It is the first cocktail book known to have included a recipe for the Old-Fashioned. In it, he lists two recipes for the drink: the first method, ironically, primarily illustrates what Old-Fashioned drinkers were trying to get away from—whiskey cocktails pimped up with things like absinthe. His second method is closer to the simplified drink the Old-Fashioned would become. Both recipes have been adapted.

METHOD NO. 1

Take a teaspoon of sugar, and dissolve it with a barspoon of water in an Old-Fashioned glass. Add Angostura bitters, a barspoon of simple syrup, and a dash of absinthe. Twist a lemon peel over mixture and drop in glass. Add two ounces of whiskey and two or three pieces of ice. Stir until chilled. Strain into chilled Old-Fashioned glass.

METHOD NO. 2

Take a teaspoon of sugar, and dissolve it with a barspoon of water in an Old-Fashioned glass. Add Angostura bitters and a barspoon of simple syrup. Twist a lemon peel over mixture and drop in glass. Add two ounces of whiskey and one large chunk of ice. Stir until chilled.

THE SAVOY OLD-FASHIONED

HARRY CRADDOCK, *THE SAVOY COCKTAIL BOOK*, 1930

In writing *The Savoy Cocktail Book*, London-based barman Harry Craddock collected and chronicled a great many cocktail recipes that might have otherwise been lost to Prohibition. Hence, Craddock's recipe may have been the very Old-Fashioned that many Americans encountered as, bleary-eyed and thirsty, they exited Prohibition. Note the recommendation of Canadian Club whisky—among the best available at the time—and a slice of orange. For the "lump" of sugar, a sugar cube will do. A "glass" of whiskey is 2 ounces. If you'd rather have rye than Canadian whisky, Old Overholt is a good and period-appropriate way to go.

1 lump sugar

2 dashes Angostura bitters

1 glass rye or Canadian Club whisky

Crush sugar and bitters together, add lump of ice, decorate with twist of lemon peel and slice of orange using medium size glass, and stir well.

BURKE'S OLD-FASHIONED

**HARMAN BURNEY BURKE, *BURKE'S COMPLETE
COCKTAIL & DRINKING RECIPES*, 1934**

This is the first-known printed rendition of the Old-Fashioned to call for muddled—or "mull"-ed—fruit. It's a style of Old-Fashioned cocktail building that would dominate the second half of the twentieth century. For purists, Burke's formula marks the beginning of a very dark age for the drink. Burke also throws much of the kitchen sink (curaçao, absinthe) in there. A sign of the times to come, après Prohibition. If you wish to include them, add them before the whiskey; just a drop or two of both will do. For the whiskey, "1 glass" is 2 ounces. Though it's not mentioned by Burke, do add ice to the cocktail and stir until chilled before serving.

Whiskey, 1 glass
Sugar, 1 lump
Angostura bitters, 2 dashes
Curacao or Absinthe, 2 dashes

Add one Slice of Orange, one Slice of Lemon Peel, mull with the Bitters and Sugar, then add the Whiskey and serve in the same glass.

THE STANDARD VARIATIONS

These recipes—beginning, of course, with the Whiskey Old-Fashioned—are so common that no bartender can claim authorship of them. Examples of a few of these can be found in cocktail books published more than a century ago, and, as evidence of their durability, they have become newly popular today. Aside from the comparatively fussy Wisconsin-style Brandy Old-Fashioned, they are all simple variations on the standard rubric of spirit-bitters-water-sugar and illustrate the innate adaptability of the formula.

RYE/BOURBON OLD-FASHIONED

Today's widespread experimentation notwithstanding, when you're talking about an authentic Old-Fashioned, the central debate is always this: rye or bourbon. In the late 1800s and early 1900s, preferences were probably fairly evenly split and depended heavily on region. In the decades after Prohibition, bourbon slowly but surely developed an edge, and rye, thought old-fashioned and somewhat disreputable (*The Lost Weekend*, etc.), fell into eclipse. In recent years, rye has made a big comeback, so drinkers once again have a choice. Doctrinaire purists tend to insist on rye, thinking it the more historically authentic choice, but both function admirably. Simply put, bourbon will give you a mellower and sweeter cocktail, whereas rye will deliver a bit more spice and kick. Among American whiskeys that provide the best value for their price—and make an outstanding Old-Fashioned—I recommend Elijah Craig 12-year and Henry McKenna single barrel (make sure it's the bonded) bourbons, and Rittenhouse 100-proof and Bulleit ryes. (McKenna, which can be difficult to find outside Kentucky, strikes a nice balance, spicewise, between the Elijah Craig and Rittenhouse).

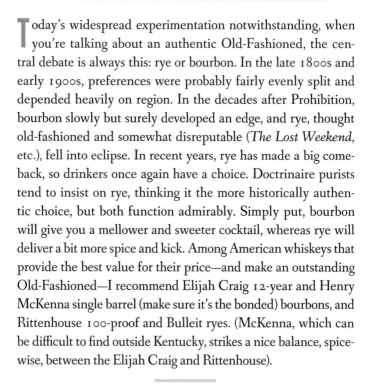

2 ounces rye or bourbon

1 sugar cube

2 dashes Angostura bitters

Orange twist

Muddle the sugar, bitters, and a barspoon of warm water at the bottom of an Old-Fashioned glass until the sugar is dissolved. Add the rye or bourbon. Stir. Add one large chunk of ice and stir until chilled. Twist a large piece of orange zest over the drink and drop into the glass.

SCOTCH OLD-FASHIONED

While rye and bourbon are the spirits of choice for a standard Old-Fashioned, a version made with Scotch is at least a century old and has its advocates. Still, it remains an oddball choice. You're one in two hundred if you order one, and very likely you love your chosen brand of Scotch a trifle more than you cherish the Old-Fashioned. Historical cocktail books are particularly frustrating regarding this cocktail; they rarely specify anything other than "Scotch," never a brand or type. Since the drink emerged in the days when single malts were all but unknown on American soil, blended Scotch—Famous Grouse and Bank Note do nicely—is the natural choice for a classic Scotch Old-Fashioned.

2 ounces blended Scotch

1 sugar cube

2 dashes Angostura bitters

Orange twist

Muddle the sugar, bitters, and a barspoon of warm water at the bottom of an Old-Fashioned glass until the sugar is dissolved. Add the Scotch. Stir. Add one large chunk of ice and stir until chilled. Twist a large piece of orange zest over the drink and drop into the glass.

RUM OLD-FASHIONED

With the recent rise of rum as a quality spirit as well as the return of the tiki bar, Old-Fashioned variations using rum are now common. For my money, no spirit outside bourbon and rye works as well within the Old-Fashioned template. The simple framing is a perfect showcase for the depth and complexity of flavor you'll find in a beautifully wrought aged rum. The Guatemalan solera-aged Zacapa is arguably the ne plus ultra for this particular drink. But the Ron Abuelo 7-year from Panama works very well, too, and is perhaps not as overwhelmingly opulent. Also excellent for this drink are the El Dorado 8-year, made in Guyana. That said, the recipe I include here comes from bartender St. John Frizell, who owns Fort Defiance, a fine bar in the Red Hook section of Brooklyn. Frizell is a fan of English Harbour rum. If you can't find the excellent Clement cane syrup, which hails from Martinique, you may want to experiment with the sweetener. Molasses is a natural companion to rum. But go easy—a half-barspoon should suffice. Otherwise, a rich Demerara syrup will do.

2 ounces English Harbour 5-year rum

1 barspoon Clement cane syrup

2 dashes Angostura bitters

Lime twist

Mix the syrup and bitters at the bottom of an Old-Fashioned glass and add the rum. Stir. Add one large chunk of ice and stir until chilled. Twist a large piece of lime zest over the drink and drop into the glass.

GENEVER OLD-FASHIONED

Over the past few years, genever, also known as Dutch or Holland gin, has become widely available in the United States. A malty, sweetish, full-bodied liquor, it is closer in character to whiskey than it is to London dry gin. Sampling this drink you'll understand why Gin Cocktails (that is, genever, sugar, bitters, and water) were once so popular. Bols is the genever that is most readily available in the United States. If you can find the headier, more full-bodied barrel-aged Bols (which tastes very similar to the Corenwijn, which is sold in Europe, but unavailable here), use it. Also, perhaps due to the fruity, floral character of the Genever, this is the one Old-Fashioned variation that actually benefits from the 1870s bartender habit of adding a dash of this or that. Shake in a drop of absinthe, curaçao, maraschino liqueur, or all three. It's all for the good.

2 ounces Bols barrel-aged genever

1 sugar cube

2 dashes Angostura bitters

Lemon twist

Muddle the sugar, bitters, and a barspoon of warm water at the bottom of an Old-Fashioned glass until the sugar is dissolved. Add the genever. Stir. Add one large chunk of ice and stir until chilled. Twist a large piece of lemon zest over the drink and drop into the glass.

APPLEJACK OLD-FASHIONED

A pplejack—that is, apple brandy—has been made in America since before the Revolution. Applejack cocktails were common in early cocktail books and, no surprise, the liquor makes for a wonderful Old-Fashioned. The bartenders of the nineteenth century probably used the applejack brand recommended here, Laird's, the oldest licensed distillery in the United States. Make sure you used the bonded version.

2 ounces Laird's bonded applejack
1 barspoon Grade B maple syrup
2 dashes Fee Brothers whiskey barrel–aged bitters
Orange twist

Mix the syrup and bitters at the bottom of an Old-Fashioned glass. Add the applejack. Stir. Add one large chunk of ice and stir until chilled. Twist a large piece of orange zest over the drink and drop into the glass.

Wisconsin Style
BRANDY OLD-FASHIONED, "SWEET"

THE OLD FASHIONED, MADISON, WI

When it comes to the Wisconsin-style Brandy Old-Fashioned, if you've had one, you know what you're getting into. It's a sweet, fruity soup, devoid of much delicacy. But love it or hate it, you've got to pay the old girl some respect. This version of the Old-Fashioned, or something close to it, has been served in the Midwest nearly nonstop since the end of Prohibition (see sidebar on page 54). As John Dye, the owner of the classic Milwaukee bar Bryant's Cocktail Lounge, states, "I am pretty sure that Wisconsin is solely responsible for keeping Angostura in business during the dark years of cocktails when most people thought an exotic cocktail consisted of Midori and sour mix."

Context is all with this cocktail. If you're in a midwestern bar, you could feel as if you're drinking the king of cocktails. If not, you may just conclude that there's no accounting for taste. But there's nothing quite like ordering like the locals when you're in Wisconsin.

This recipe comes from the Madison bar and restaurant The Old-Fashioned, which sells hundreds of its namesake cocktail every day. Using Korbel is important if you want to drink authentically. But, if you can't locate a bottle, another light-bodied domestic brandy will do. This is one Old-Fashioned that I recommend be drunk not only prior to a meal, but also with it. Preferably, that meal should be prime rib or a Friday-night fish fry.

continued

2 ounces Korbel brandy

1 sugar cube

4 dashes Angostura bitters

2 orange slices

2 maraschino cherries

7-Up or Sprite

In an Old-Fashioned glass, combine the sugar, bitters, 1 of the orange slices, 1 of the cherries, stemmed, and a splash of 7-Up. Muddle the ingredients. Fill the glass with ice cubes and add the brandy. Stir until chilled. Top with 7-Up and garnish with the remaining orange slice and cherry.

MODERN CLASSICS

These drinks, all of recent vintage, date from the headiest years of the (continuing) cocktail renaissance. Once the Old-Fashioned was reestablished as a classic cocktail worthy of adulation, it soon became regarded as a cocktail worthy of imitation—which, as we are constantly told, is a form of flattery. Some of these drinks were created as calling cards for new bars, some as advertisements for the versatility of a spirit. A few are a vehicle for a new drink-building technique, while still others are flights of fancy that somehow landed on all fours. All are delicious.

OAXACA OLD-FASHIONED

PHIL WARD, DEATH & CO, MANHATTAN, 2007

Along with Don Lee's Benton's Old-Fashioned (page 106), this is the most renowned of the twenty-first-century variations of the Old-Fashioned, and one of the modern cocktail era's gateway drinks into the pleasures of tequila and mezcal. It was invented in 2007 by New York–based mixologist Phil Ward, when he was working behind the bar at Death & Co, one of the earliest and most influential of the Manhattan cocktail dens that cropped up in the first decade of this century. Since then the drink has become a popular addition to cocktail menus around the world. Says Ward, "The Oaxaca Old-Fashioned was my epiphany drink: 'Holy shit, this stuff works!'" The stuff was mezcal, tequila's smokier, rough-hewn cousin, and in this drink it transformed something so simple and basic into something of much greater results than the sum of its parts. The choice of spirits brands here is critical—both El Tesoro and Del Maguey are superior expressions of their spirits—as is the use of agave nectar instead of sugar.

1 ½ ounces El Tesoro reposado tequila
½ ounce Del Maguey single village mezcal
(Chichicapa or San Luis del Rio)
2 dashes Angostura bitters
1 barspoon agave nectar
Orange twist

Combine all the ingredients except the orange twist in an Old-Fashioned glass filled with one large ice cube. Stir until chilled. To top with a flamed orange twist, hold a piece of orange peel about the size of a silver dollar, skin side down, over the drink. Light a match and use it to warm the skin side of the peel. Holding the match a few inches above the drink, quickly squeeze the peel in the direction of the match. The oil from the peel will briefly erupt into flame, showering its essence over the drink's surface.

BENTON'S OLD-FASHIONED

DON LEE, PDT, MANHATTAN, 2007

Though barman Eben Freeman—who worked at chef Wylie Dufresne's WD-50 and Sam Mason's Tailor, both in New York—had previously experimented with the process of fat washing (infusing alcohol with the flavor of fats like butter or bacon fat) to make cocktails, this was the drink that opened people's eyes to the possibilities in combining flesh and firewater. It's been wildly popular from the day it was introduced at the Manhattan neo-speakeasy PDT. (It remains PDT's top seller, week in and week out.) Dozens of savory cocktails have followed in the path it blazed, though few have matched it for sheer deliciousness.

---

2 ounces Benton's Bacon Fat–Infused Bourbon (page 107)

¼ ounce Grade B maple syrup

2 dashes Angostura bitters

Orange twist

Combine all the ingredients except the orange twist in an Old-Fashioned glass. Stir over one large ice cube until chilled. Twist a large piece of orange zest over the drink and drop into the glass.

BENTON'S BACON FAT–INFUSED BOURBON

MAKES 750 ML

1 ½ ounces bacon fat

1 (750 ml) bottle Four Roses bourbon

Warm the bacon fat in a small saucepan on over low heat, stirring until it is melted, about 5 minutes. Combine the melted fat with the bourbon in a large freezer-safe container and stir. Cover and let sit at room temperature for 4 hours, then place the container in the freezer for 2 hours. Remove the solid fat from the surface of the bourbon and discard. Strain the bourbon through a terry cloth towel or a double layer of cheesecloth into a bottle and store in the refrigerator for up to 2 months.

PRIME MEATS OLD-FASHIONED

DAMON BOELTE, PRIME MEATS, BROOKLYN, 2009

When Prime Meats opened on a corner of Court Street in Carroll Gardens, Brooklyn, in 2009, bar manager Damon Boelte found the key ingredient to the house Old-Fashioned in a courtyard behind the restaurant: an old Bartlett pear tree. Since then, he has annually made bitters from the fruit, bitters that lend the cocktail an unusual, bright edge. Making your own bitters is a time investment, but a pleasant one and, in terms of end result, worth the trouble. The recipe that follows, which is Damon's own, also appears in the book *Bitters*. The various ingredients can be found at any store that specializes in bulk or exotic spices, such as Kalustyan's in Manhattan. Turbinado is a less-refined, sugar cane–based coarse sugar, easily found at boutique grocery and health food stores; to make turbinado syrup, follow the instructions for simple syrup on page 73.

2 ounces Rittenhouse 100-proof rye

¼ ounce turbinado syrup (see instructions for simple syrup on page 73)

3 dashes Bartlett Pear Bitters (page 110)

Lemon twist

Combine all the ingredients except the lemon twist in a mixing glass filled with ice. Stir until chilled. Strain over one large chunk of ice in an Old-Fashioned glass. Twist a large piece of lemon zest over the drink and drop into the glass.

continued

BARTLETT PEAR BITTERS

MAKES ABOUT 20 OUNCES

3 Bartlett pears, cored and coarsely chopped

Zest of 1 lemon, cut into strips with a paring knife

1 cinnamon stick

¼ teaspoon allspice berries

½ teaspoon black peppercorns

½ teaspoon cinchona bark

¼ teaspoon calamus root

4 cloves

1 vanilla bean, halved lengthwise and seeds
scraped out (use both pod and seeds)

3-inch piece of fresh ginger, peeled and coarsely chopped

2 cups high-proof vodka, plus more if needed

1 cup water

2 tablespoons simple syrup (page 73)

Place all of the ingredients except the vodka, water, and simple syrup in a large Mason jar. Pour in the 2 cups vodka, adding more if necessary until the contents of the jar are covered. Seal the jar and store at room temperature out of direct sunlight for 2 weeks, shaking the jar once a day. After 2 weeks, strain the liquid through a cheesecloth-lined funnel into a clean quart jar. Repeat, if necessary, until all the sediment has been filtered out. Transfer the solids to a small saucepan. Cover the jar and set aside. Cover the solids with the 1 cup of water and bring to a boil. Cover the saucepan, lower the heat, and simmer for 10 minutes. Let cool. Add all contents of the saucepan to a quart-size Mason

jar. Cover and store at room temperature for one week, shaking the jar daily. After one week, strain the jar with the liquid and solids through a funnel lined with cheesecloth into another clean quart Mason jar. Repeat straining until all sediment is filtered out. Discard the solids. Add the liquid to Mason jar containing the original vodka solution. Add the syrup to the solution. Stir, then cover, then shake to fully dissolve. Allow mixture to stand at room temperature for three days. Skim off any debris that floats to the surface. Strain through cheesecloth a final time. Using a funnel, decant bitters into smaller jars and label. Bitters will last indefinitely.

ELDER FASHIONED

PHIL WARD, DEATH & CO, MANHATTAN, 2007

A nother Old-Fashioned variation from Phil Ward, this one features London dry gin. This drink was created around the time that the elderflower liqueur St-Germain was introduced. The liqueur took the bartending world by storm, introducing a new flavor to the mixologist's palette. But because it became so ubiquitous on cocktail menus, it quickly became known somewhat derisively as "bartender's ketchup." That history doesn't detract from the simple, sweet appeal of this floral, fruity cocktail. It is the lightest and summeriest of Old-Fashioneds, while sneakily still packing the alcoholic punch of any other version of the drink.

2 ounces Plymouth gin

½ ounce St-Germain elderflower liqueur

2 dashes orange bitters

Grapefruit twist

Combine all the ingredients except the grapefruit twist in an Old-Fashioned glass. Add one large chunk of ice and stir until chilled. Twist a piece of grapefruit zest over the drink and drop into the glass.

CONFERENCE

BRIAN MILLER, DEATH & CO, MANHATTAN, 2007

M iller created this cocktail for one of the waitresses at Death & Co, as her "shift drink" one evening. "Using an Old-Fashioned template, I took four of my favorite spirits at the time—this was before I became a rumhead—and blended them all together," Miller recalls. "The drink wasn't perfect the first time I served it, but after finding the perfect bitters combination (the Bittermens mole was the key), I was home free." The name comes from a 1973 episode of the TV show *M*A*S*H* called "Deal Me Out." In an early scene, prior to a "conference" (really a poker game), an officer is offered "Scotch, gin, vodka—for your convenience, all in the same bottle."

The mix of liquors here—actually two whiskies and two brandies—leads to a fetching and surprisingly subtle complexity. It is, indeed, not a battle of spirits but a civilized conference, one in which an assembly of grains and grapes and fruits peaceably convene to talk things out. It may just be me, but I suspect the calvados and cognac have the slight upper hand in this flavor confab. It wouldn't be the first time the French outtalked everyone else.

½ ounce Rittenhouse 100-proof rye

½ ounce Buffalo Trace bourbon

½ ounce Busnel VSOP calvados

½ ounce Hine H cognac

1 teaspoon Demerara syrup (page 73)

2 dashes Angostura bitters

1 dash Bittermens Xocolatl mole bitters

Orange twist

Lemon twist

Combine all the ingredients except the orange and lemon twists in an Old-Fashioned glass. Add one large chunk of ice and stir until chilled. Twist a large piece of orange zest and a large piece of lemon zest over the drink and drop into the glass.

ALBINO OLD-FASHIONED

TAD CARDUCCI, BAR CELONA, BROOKLYN, 2009

I first tasted this drink at Bar Celona, in the Brooklyn neighborhood of Williamsburg. At the time, so-called white whiskey—unaged whiskey straight off the still, also known as white dog—was a commercial oddity. The Death's Door product, out of Wisconsin, was one of the first on the market. Its pungent, chewy nature was a revelation, and the character of the grain came through strongly. Today, now that every major whiskey brand seems to sell an unaged version, the novelty has worn off, but this remains an excellent drink that nicely showcases the attractions of the raw spirit. "We wanted to create something very simple to entice both seasoned whiskey drinkers and lovers of white spirits alike," Carducci said of this cocktail. You may want to remove the grapefruit wedge after muddling it, as it tends to get in the way of one's drinking. Homemade brandied cherries are very easy to make. But, in lieu of that, the commercially sold Luxardo cherries will do nicely.

2 ounces Death's Door white whiskey

½ ounce simple syrup (page 73)

2 brandied cherries

1 wedge white grapefruit

2 dashes Angostura bitters

Muddle the cherries and grapefruit in the bottom of a heavy Old-Fashioned glass. Add the remaining ingredients and one large chunk of ice and stir until chilled.

 HIGHLANDER

ERIC ALPERIN, THE VARNISH, LOS ANGELES, 2010

A lperin says of this Scotch-based drink, it's "so simple that I thought I couldn't be proud of it, but my guests love to order it." Simplicity can be a wonderful thing when you're parched and weary on a Friday night at the end of a long week. And there's no Old-Fashioned recipe in this book as simple as this one. There are no bitters, and the Cherry Heering, a widely available Danish liqueur made from cherries and various spices, provides the sweetening agent (and, in liquid form, the cherry garnish). Go big on the lemon twist. It brightens the whole thing.

2 ounces blended Scotch, such as Bank Note or Famous Grouse

½ ounce Cherry Heering

Lemon twist

Combine the Scotch and Cherry Heering in an Old-Fashioned glass. Add one large chunk of ice and stir until chilled. Twist a large piece of lemon zest over the drink and drop into the glass.

THE CLINT EASTWOOD

MIKE RYAN, THE VIOLET HOUR, CHICAGO, 2009

Mike Ryan is certainly not the first bartender to try adding a little Chartreuse to his Whiskey Cocktail. They were pulling that stunt back in the 1870s. It was one of the "improvements" that drove drinkers to pine for simpler times. But, tasting this drink, you may wonder what they were complaining about. The double herbal hit of this drink, furnished by the Chartreuse and the heavy dose of Angostura bitters, may remind you of bitters' early rep as a medicinal cure. One can picture Clint's Man with No Name squinting and baring his front teeth after drawing on one of these.

Served up, Ryan's potion may fool you into thinking you're having a riff on the Manhattan. Indeed, this drink splits the difference between the Old-Fashioned and the Manhattan. I've tried it on the rocks, though, too, and it doesn't suffer for the change.

---

2 ounces rye whiskey

⅛ ounce (approximately ¾ teaspoon) Angostura bitters

⅛ ounce (approximately ¾ teaspoon) green Chartreuse

¼ ounce Demerara syrup (page 73)

Orange twist

Combine all the ingredients except the orange twist in a mixing glass filled with ice and stir until chilled. Strain into a chilled cocktail glass and serve up. Cut a piece of orange peel and lightly squeeze its oils atop the cocktail.

HONEY-NUT OLD-FASHIONED

MARCOS TELLO, 1886 BAR, PASADENA, CALIFORNIA, 2010

This is a perfect Old-Fashioned for anyone with a serious sweet tooth (or caught in an arrested state of adolescence). The name hits it on the head: if you've ever eaten Honey Nut Cheerios for breakfast, you'll recognize the flavor profile. Instead of General Mills's classic oat loops, however, bourbon does the duty as the grain in this recipe. Regarding the nuts, Tellos says, "It pays to invest in good dry-roasted peanuts, as this means more oils, and you will definitely get a fat cap off them when you freeze the infusion." Translation: No Planters.

---

2 ounces Peanut-Infused Bourbon (page 123)

¼ ounce Honey Syrup (page 123)

1 dash Angostura bitters

Orange twist

Combine all the ingredients except the orange twist in an Old-Fashioned glass with ice and stir until chilled. Twist a large piece of orange zest over the drink and drop into the glass.

PEANUT-INFUSED BOURBON

MAKES 1½ CUPS

1 cup unsalted dry-roasted peanuts

1 ½ cups Elijah Craig 12-year bourbon

Combine the peanuts and bourbon in a nonreactive container, cover, and leave at room temperature for 24 hours. Strain through a double layer of cheesecloth into a clean freezer-safe container and place in the freezer for 24 hours. Scrape away the solid fat from the surface of the liquid and discard. Let the mixture warm to room temperature, then strain through a double layer of cheesecloth into a clean bottle. The bourbon will keep for a week.

HONEY SYRUP

MAKES 1 CUP

1 cup clover honey

⅓ cup hot water

Combine the ingredients in a bowl and stir to dissolve the honey. Stored tightly sealed in the refrigerator, the syrup will keep for 1 week.

THE REBENNACK

CHRIS HANNAH, FRENCH 75 BAR, NEW ORLEANS, 2009

I t's easy to see that a New Orleans bartender came up with this one: every ingredient screams "Big Easy." Rye, the foundation of the Sazerac, has long been a New Orleans favorite; Clement's rum-based orange liqueur is said to be based on a historic Creole recipe; the Amaro Averna speaks to NOLA's Italian heritage; and Peychaud's is the Crescent City's own bitters. (With a little searching, the Clement Creole Shrubb is easily located in most cities.) Even the unusual choice of glassware is a nod to the city's historic love of French brandy. The snifter is appropriate since this is a very elegant drink, its many interesting facets smoothed over by a silky texture. The cocktail is titled after the surname of beloved New Orleans musician Dr. John.

---

1 ¾ ounces rye
¾ ounce Amaro Averna
¼ ounce Clement Creole Shrubb
3 dashes Peychaud's bitters
Orange peel

Combine all the ingredients except the orange twist in a mixing glass filled with ice and stir until chilled. Strain into an ice-filled brandy snifter. To make the garnish, cut several thin strands of orange peel and tie them together with another strand of orange peel, then drop into glass.

THE SMOKING GUN

LYNNETTE MARRERO, 2010

Marrero created this drink for the 2010 Metropolitan Opera Cocktail Competition, an annual mixology contest organized by the opera-loving Brooklyn distiller Allen Katz. The name is a nod to the opera that was presented the night of the competition, Puccini's *The Girl of the Golden West*. The smoke of this smoking gun is furnished by a special simple syrup infused with Lapsang souchong tea. The earthy, herbal notes of the CioCiaro, a bittersweet Italian digestif, contribute to the wild edge of the cocktail while lending an appropriate Italian element to the mix. A cooling bit of campfire in a glass.

1½ ounces Rittenhouse rye
¼ ounce Amaro CioCiaro
¼ ounce Smoked Demerara Syrup (page 127)
1 dash Bittermens Xocolatl mole bitters
1 dash Angostura bitters
Orange twist

Combine all the ingredients except the orange twist in an Old-Fashioned glass. Add one large chunk of ice and stir until chilled. To top with a flamed orange twist, hold a piece of orange peel about the size of a silver dollar, skin side down, over the drink. Light a match and use it to warm the skin side of the peel. Holding the match a few inches above the drink, quickly squeeze the peel in the direction of the match. The oil from the peel will briefly erupt into flame, showering its essence over the drink's surface.

SMOKED DEMERARA SYRUP

MAKES ABOUT 1¹/₂ CUPS

1 tablespoon loose Lapsang souchong tea leaves

1 cup boiling water

1 cup Demerara syrup (page 73)

Combine the tea and water in a small saucepan and let steep for 2 hours. Stain the tea leaves with a fine-mesh sieve, add the Demerara syrup to the liquid, and bring to a simmer over medium heat. Simmer until reduced by one quarter. Let cool before using. Stored tightly sealed in the refrigerator, the syrup will keep for 1 week.

BLACK WALNUT OLD-FASHIONED

**TOBY MALONEY, BRADSTREET
CRAFTSHOUSE, MINNEAPOLIS, 2009**

Bartender and cocktail consultant Toby Maloney says that, in creating this drink, he wanted "to do an Old-Fashioned that was simple and elegant (in the land of muddled abominations) and really dry with a velvety mouth feel." Because of the walnut liqueur—a rich spirit made from unripe walnuts, traditional to the Alpine regions of Germany, Austria, and Italy—used to rinse the glass prior to filling it, this is one of the few cocktails in this book that is built in a mixing glass, not the serving glass. The use of the Nux Alpina and the choice of orange over Angostura bitters mark the only shifts away from the classic Old-Fashioned formula here. But they are difference enough, adding an elegant nutty finish to the drink.

2 ounces Bulleit bourbon

¼ ounce Demerara syrup (page 73)

3 dashes orange bitters

Nux Alpina black walnut liqueur

Orange twist

Combine the bourbon, Demerara syrup, and bitters in a mixing glass filled with ice and stir until chilled. Rinse an Old-Fashioned glass with the black walnut liqueur. Add one large ice cube. Strain the contents of the mixing glass into the Old-Fashioned glass. Twist a large piece of orange zest over the drink and drop into the glass.

NUEVO VIEJO

**JON SANTER, PRIZEFIGHTER,
EMERYVILLE, CALIFORNIA, 2011**

This simple drink is a good illustration of how a slight variation in the simple building blocks of the Old-Fashioned can vastly alter the resulting drink. In outline, this is easily recognizable as an Old-Fashioned. But in character, it stands apart from its mainstream brother. The Bank Note blended Scotch—an excellent whiskey considering its very affordable price—is meaty and gamy, lacking the toasty sweet notes of bourbon. The rich maple syrup contributes to the vaguely outdoorsy feel of the cocktail. It's a broad, boisterous Old-Fashioned with a lot of stick-to-your-ribs body. You'd want this in your camp after a day of deer hunting.

If you can't locate Miracle Mile bitters, which are produced in Los Angeles, Scrappy's aromatic bitters and Bitter Truth aromatic bitters are recommended as substitutes.

***

2 ounces Bank Note blended Scotch

¼ ounce Grade B maple syrup

2 dashes Miracle Mile forbidden bitters

Orange twist

Combine the Scotch, maple syrup, and bitters in an Old-Fashioned glass. Add one large chunk of ice and stir until chilled. Twist a large piece of orange zest over the drink and drop into the glass.

THE AGAVE COCKTAIL

ERICK CASTRO, BOURBON & BRANCH, SAN FRANCISCO, 2008

"This cocktail works as well as it does mostly because El Jimador is aged in brand-new charred oak barrels much like bourbon," explains Castro. "The cinnamon in place of the more common twist gives it a little something different." The cinnamon garnish used here indeed sets this cocktail apart from its fellows, lending it a toasty, comforting note. If it happens to be raining outside, you may just extract a little extra solace from each sip.

2 ounces El Jimador añejo tequila

1 barspoon agave nectar

2 dashes Angostura bitters

Freshly grated cinnamon, for garnish

Combine the tequila, agave nectar, and bitters in an Old-Fashioned glass. Add one large chunk of ice and stir until chilled. Garnish with grated cinnamon.

MALACCA OLD-FASHIONED

BOBBY HEUGEL, ANVIL BAR & REFUGE, HOUSTON, 2010

Malacca was a softer style of gin that Tanqueray released in 1997. It didn't catch on, though, and it slowly vanished from liquor store shelves. A few years later mixologists realized that the lost Malacca was the probably just the thing for all the nineteenth-century cocktail recipes they were trying to re-create that called for Old Tom gin. Tanqueray finally responded in 2013 with a one-time-only run of Malacca. "It's a pretty basic cocktail," says Heugel, "as I was asked to make a drink with a limited supply of the Malacca before the rerelease. I tried to really just showcase the gin without altering it much." If Tanqueray stays true to their word, the Malacca supply will eventually run out. When and if that happens, you can swap in the sweeter but similar Hayman's Old Tom gin, which is here to stay.

2 ounces Tanqueray Malacca gin

1 barspoon Demerara syrup (page 73)

2 dashes Peychaud's bitters

1 dash Angostura orange bitters

Lemon twist

Combine all the ingredients except the lemon twist in an Old-Fashioned glass. Add one large chunk of ice and stir until chilled. Twist a large piece of lemon zest over the drink and drop into the glass.

CLIFF OLD-FASHIONED

BOOKER AND DAX, MANHATTAN, 2012

B ooker and Dax is a high-tech cocktail bar in the East Village where few drinks make it to the customer without first passing through some scientific process or contraption. This lovely spicy drink, which was actually created before the bar opened for business, is one of the bar's simpler creations. Both the Yamazaki and Rittenhouse work well, but I prefer the former, as the smooth polish of the Japanese single malt plays nicely against the spicy coriander and red pepper syrup.

2 ounces whiskey, preferably Yamazaki 12-year
single malt or Rittenhouse 100-proof rye

Scant ½ ounce Coriander Syrup (page 135)

2 dashes Angostura bitters

Orange twist

Combine all the ingredients except the orange twist in an Old-Fashioned glass. Add one large chunk of ice and stir until chilled. Twist a large piece of orange zest over the drink and drop into the glass.

CORIANDER SYRUP

MAKES ABOUT ½ CUP

Scant ½ cup water

Scant ½ cup sugar

3 teaspoons coriander seeds

1½ teaspoons crushed red pepper

Combine the water, sugar, coriander seeds, and ½ teaspoon of the crushed red pepper in a medium saucepan. Bring to a boil, turn off the heat, then add the remaining 1 teaspoon crushed red pepper. Stir and let steep, tasting occasionally, until the flavor of the spices in the syrup hits the back of your throat but does not overwhelm the mixture. Strain through a double layer of cheesecloth or fine-mesh chinois, then let cool before using. Stored tightly sealed in the refrigerator, the syrup will keep for 1 week.

YOU'RE TURNING VIOLET, VIOLET

LYNN HOUSE, BLACKBIRD, CHICAGO, 2013

This may rank as the most unusual Old-Fashioned in this book. I had never known what to do with the Utah-based distillery High West's pungent and volatile oat whiskey until Chicago's Lynn House passed this improbable recipe along. The sweet, bright blueberry preserves tame the grain, while the lively spices of the Creole bitters somehow meet the two in the middle. (House makes her own blueberry preserves for this drink, though she says high-quality store-bought preserves will do. But "no Smucker's.") The lemon juice lends a needed snap of acidity while also pushing the drink into Whiskey Sour territory. It's one of those cocktails that works in spite of its motley crew of ingredients.

Appropriately, the name of this cocktail quotes the movie *Willy Wonka and the Chocolate Factory*, an adaptation of a Roald Dahl story about a wizard of confections. If Wonka had been a mixologist, he might have come up with a cocktail like this one.

2 ounces High West Silver oat whiskey

½ ounce fresh lemon juice

3 teaspoons blueberry preserves

3 dashes Bitter Truth Creole bitters

Blueberries, for garnish

Combine all the ingredients except the blueberries an ice-filled cocktail shaker. Shake and strain into an Old-Fashioned glass over one large ice cube. Garnish with fresh blueberries.

MUNICH OLD-FASHIONED

FRANK CISNEROS, BOURGEOIS PIG, BROOKLYN, 2011

F rank Cisneros created this drink for the opening menu at the Bourgeois Pig, a short-lived bar in Brooklyn. "I wanted to approach classic and often forgotten continental spirits the way an American bartender from the golden age might have approached them," said Cisneros. "So proportionally, you've got the same formula of sweet to bitter to spiritous but mixed up with German brandy and honey liqueur and an Austrian eau de vie. I thought about incorporating a more obtuse European bitter but sometimes nothing beats Angostura, and I think sticking to a theme too literally can be a detriment to an otherwise good drink."

2 ounces Asbach Uralt brandy

1 ½ teaspoons Rothman & Winter orchard apricot liqueur

1 teaspoon Bärenjäger honey liqueur

3 dashes Angostura bitters

Lemon twist

Orange twist

Combine all the ingredients except the twists in an Old-Fashioned glass. Add one large chunk of ice and stir until chilled. Twist a large piece of lemon zest and a large piece of orange zest over the drink and drop into the glass.

McKITTRICK OLD-FASHIONED

THEO LIEBERMAN, MILK & HONEY, MANHATTAN, 2011

This drink was inspired by the stage show *Sleep No More*. An atmospheric, interactive take on *Macbeth* created by the British theater group Punchdrunk, it was set in the fictional McKittrick Hotel in Chelsea, New York. An unexpected hit, it became a favorite of mixologists. If the Thane of Cawdor had had a couple of these during that dinner with Duncan, he might have calmed right down and rethought his murderous plan. The rich Pedro Ximénez sherry does the job of the sugar here, and then some. Smooth and luxe, this is a good Old-Fashioned nightcap.

2 ounces bourbon

½ ounce Pedro Ximénez sherry

2 dashes mole bitters

Brandied cherry, for garnish

Combine all the ingredients except the brandied cherry in a double Old-Fashioned glass. Add a large chunk of ice and stir until chilled. Garnish with the brandied cherry.

ABSINTHE OLD-FASHIONED

DOUG PETRY, RYE, LOUISVILLE, KENTUCKY, 2012

This cocktail wasn't on the menu the night I walked into Rye, an excellent and adventurous young restaurant in Louisville's East Market District. But after a short chat with the bartender, the drink came up in conversation. I ordered it as a sort of dare, to see if it was possible that lethally strong absinthe could function as the base of an Old-Fashioned. "We wanted to do a menu based on the Old-Fashioned with the basic recipe coming down to base spirit, bittering agent, and sweetening agent," said Petry. "We wanted to try it with some spirits that weren't typical and thought absinthe would be a fun way to go with it. After a few missteps, we found a recipe that we liked and went with it." It takes an equal measure of sweet stuff—in this case a combination of simple syrup and elderflower liqueur—to tame the fiery power of the absinthe. But tame it, it does, while also nicely toning down the licorice flavor. The Peychaud's adds a needed dry note as well as provides some color to the milky green liquid. Still, don't make the mistake of drinking two of these. In fact, make it your final drink of the night. You won't need another.

1½ ounces Kübler absinthe
1 ounce simple syrup (page 73)
½ ounce St-Germain elderflower liqueur
3 or 4 dashes Peychaud's bitters

Combine the absinthe, simple syrup, and St-Germain in a mixing glass filled with ice and stir until chilled. Strain over a large chunk of ice in an Old-Fashioned glass. Float the Peychaud's bitters on top.

BELLOCQ OLD-FASHIONED COBBLER

BELLOCQ, NEW ORLEANS, 2012

The cobbler, a julep-like drink marked by a load of pebbled ice and various fruit adornments, is one of the most adaptable beverage models in cocktail history. The New Orleans bar Bellocq has proven this. Call out any liquor on their backbar, from Chartreuse to Madeira, and they'll make you a cobbler out of it. Given the Old-Fashioned's and the cobbler's shared history with fruit, it was only natural that the two would eventually come together. Says Bellocq owner Kirk Estopinal, the drink takes its cue from the "muddled-style Old-Fashioned, the kind you used to get everywhere before the mixology movement took hold." The result doesn't taste very different from an Old-Fashioned with muddled fruit, just a lot more refreshing. The vanilla and powdered sugar turn the fruit "flag" into a candied postdrink treat.

2 ounces Buffalo Trace bourbon

¼ ounce Demerara syrup (page 73)

2 dashes Angostura bitters

*1 orange wheel (½ inch thick), plus ¼ orange
wheel (½ inch thick), for garnish*

1 Luxardo maraschino cherry, for garnish

2 drops good-quality vanilla extract

Powdered sugar, for garnish

Muddle the orange wheel at the bottom of a mixing glass. Add the bourbon, Demerara syrup, and bitters. Fill with ice and shake well. Strain into a julep cup or a collins glass filled with cracked ice. Garnish with a "flag": skewer the orange wheel quarter and cherry on a toothpick, add 2 drops of vanilla on the orange, and sprinkle with powdered sugar.

YOUNG LADDIE

JOAQUÍN SIMÓ, DEATH & CO, MANHATTAN, 2007

Single malt whiskeys are often thought to be too individualistic to play well with other ingredients. Hence, their lesser role in the classic cocktail canon. In this drink, however, Simó manages to tempt the unpeaty Islay-made Bruichladdich out onto the playground with two different forms of bright grapefruit. Other single malt Scotches can be substituted, says Simó, so long as they aren't too smoky. Be sure to go big on those twists.

2 ounces Bruichladdich "Rocks" Scotch whisky

¼ ounce simple syrup (page 73)

1 dash Peychaud's bitters

1 dash Bittermens hopped grapefruit bitters

Orange twist

Grapefruit twist

Combine all the ingredients except the twists in an Old-Fashioned glass. Add one large chunk of ice and stir until chilled. Twist a wide piece of orange zest and a wide piece of grapefruit zest over the drink and drop into the glass.

THE TREE HOUSE

JULIE REINER, LANI KAI, MANHATTAN, 2010

Julie Reiner, of New York's Flatiron Lounge and Clover Club fame, created this tiki version of an Old-Fashioned for her late, lamented tropical SoHo bar Lani Kai. The key ingredient here is the Macadamia Nut Orgeat, which functions as the sweetener and safely places this Old-Fashioned in tiki territory. A singular and superior item, the macadamia nut orgeat is produced by a Brooklyn tiki aficionado who goes by the name "Tiki Adam." (Real name: Adam Kolesar.) Kolesar began producing his orgeats commercially in 2013. They are well worth a web search (www.orgeatworks.com).

1 ounce Rittenhouse rye whiskey
1 ounce Gosling's Black Seal rum
¼ ounce macadamia nut orgeat
2 dashes Bittermens Xocolatl mole bitters

Combine all the ingredients in a mixing glass filled with ice. Stir until chilled and then strain into a chilled double Old-Fashioned glass over a single chunk of ice. If you happen to have a small umbrella or pirate-themed swizzle stick on hand, that would make an appropriate garnish.

THE NEW CEREMONY

TONIA GUFFEY, DRAM, BROOKLYN, 2013

Tonia Guffey, a regular presence at Dram, a bartender's bar in Williamsburg, Brooklyn, has a way with blending disparate liquid ingredients. Here, she makes a happy home for spicy rye, the rich, wine-based aperitif Byrrh, bright and fruity Pamplemousse and Aperol, and bone-dry vermouth. A hundred flavors dance inside this easy-to-like cocktail, which flirts as much with Manhattan model as it does with the Old-Fashioned. The name comes from a song by Dry the River, an English folk-rock band. According to Guffey, the song mysteriously comes on at Dram whenever she's making the drink.

1 ounce Rittenhouse rye

½ ounce Byrrh

½ ounce Combier Pamplemousse grapefruit liqueur

½ ounce dry vermouth

¼ ounce Aperol

3 dashes orange bitters

Grapefruit twist

Combine all the ingredients except the grapefruit twist in a double Old-Fashioned glass. Add one large chunk of ice and stir until chilled. Twist a large piece of grapefruit zest over the drink and drop into the glass.

THE GRAND BARGAIN

TOM MACY, CLOVER CLUB, BROOKLYN, 2013

This drink has actually never been offered at Clover Club. Its ingredients are luxurious—and luxuriously priced—which makes it a rather unprofitable item to serve regularly. (The drink's name, in that sense, could be considered a bit of irony.) Macy created it upon finding he had the pricy ingredients on hand at home, while recalling that mezcal and apple brandy enjoyed a peculiar affinity. The cocktail is an appropriately rich, silky experience, with notes of baked apple, smoked pear, and cherry. It may cost a pretty penny to build, but you'll go broke smiling. (For a budget version, if you must, you can use Laird's bonded applejack and Del Maguey crema mezcal.)

1½ ounces Laird's 12-year apple brandy

¾ ounces Del Maguey Santo Domingo mezcal

½ ounce Luxardo maraschino liqueur

2 dashes Angostura bitters

2 dashes Regan's orange bitters

Orange twist

Lemon twist

Combine all the ingredients except the twists in an Old-Fashioned glass. Add one large chunk of ice and stir until chilled. Twist a large piece of orange zest and a large piece of lemon zest over the drink and drop into the glass.

GRAND FASHIONED

JASON KOSMAS, EMPLOYEES ONLY, MANHATTAN, 1999

This drink was actually created years before Kosmas helped found Employees Only, the wildly popular Greenwich Village cocktail lounge. It won first place at a Grand Marnier cocktail contest in 1999. Kosmas's goal was to create a drink that used two full ounces of the orange liqueur without ending up with an unbearably sweet drink. To turn this trick, he incorporated muddled blood oranges and plenty of tart lime juice. It's a still a sweet drink, but a complex one.

---

2 ounces Grand Marnier

1 teaspoon sugar

3 dashes Angostura bitters

3 blood orange wedges, peeled

¾ ounce lime juice

Combine the sugar, bitters, and blood orange wedges in the bottom of a mixing glass and muddle. Add the Grand Marnier and lime juice, fill the glass with ice, and shake hard and briefly. Pour entire contents into a chilled Old-Fashioned glass.

THE SEXTANT

DUSTIN KNOX, CENTRAL, PORTLAND, OREGON, 2010

This is basically an aquavit Old-Fashioned. Aquavit, the traditional Scandinavian spirit that's just a few savory seeds away from vodka, has flavors of caraway and anise. Knox prefers the limited-release aged Gammal Krogstad aquavit from House Spirits, a fine Portland-based distillery, but he says that company's unaged Krogstad aquavit also works quite well.

2 ounces barrel-aged Gammal Krogstad aquavit

½ barspoon Grade B maple syrup

1 dash Fee Brothers whiskey barrel–aged bitters

Grapefruit twist

Star anise

Before you make the drink, light one star anise aflame with a match or lighter on a wooden surface or cutting board. Then invert an Old-Fashioned glass over the smoldering embers to wash it in the smoke. Combine the aquavit, maple syrup, and bitters in a mixing glass filled with ice and stir until chilled. Strain into the smoky glass over one large ice cube. Twist a large piece of grapefruit zest over the drink and drop into the glass.

THE HAUNTED HOUSE

JEREMY OERTEL, DONNA, BROOKLYN, 2011

Take a little rye, a little rum, a ginger kick, and a nice Swedish punsch (a blend of rum, sugar, spice, and Batavia arrack, an Asian liquor derived of sugar cane and red rice) and you have an extremely fun take on the Old-Fashioned. Don't misunderstand me—I have fun anytime I'm drinking the cocktail. But this version is a buoyant party starter, full of sneaky south-of-the-border spice and fruit. Without the devilishly delicious Swedish punsch (which is produced by the Minnesota-based importer Haus Alpenz and can be found at finer liquor shops), some of the life would leave the soiree, but every invitee is doing its part in this highly social mix.

"I was trying to use a lot of rum at Donna when we opened because of the Central American/Latin feel of the place," explains Oertel. The owner of Donna, Leif Huckman, is in a band called Haunted Houses, hence the name of the drink.

continued

1 ounce Appleton Estate V/X Jamaican rum

1 ounce Rittenhouse rye

½ ounce Kronan Swedish punsch

¼ ounce Ginger Syrup (see below)

2 dashes Angostura bitters

Orange twist

Combine all the ingredients except the orange twist in a mixing glass filled with ice. Stir until chilled, then strain over one large chunk of ice in an Old-Fashioned glass. Twist a large piece of orange zest over the drink and drop into the glass.

GINGER SYRUP

MAKES 1 CUP

1 cup sugar

1 (2-inch) knob fresh ginger, sliced into coins

1 cup water

Heat the sugar, ginger, and water in a saucepan over medium heat, stirring occasionally until the sugar has dissolved. The moment the water begins to boil, remove from the heat, let cool, then strain into a separate container. Stored tightly sealed in the refrigerator, the syrup will keep for 1 week.

ODE TO ADKINS

ANU APTE, ROB ROY, SEATTLE, 2010

Rob Roy, a cocktail bar in Seattle, is known for its way with an Old-Fashioned. "The drink was inspired by a drink that Erik Adkins had on the Heaven's Dog menu," says owner Anu Apte, mentioning the San Francisco bar. "When I came back to Seattle I wanted to make it for a guest but I couldn't remember the exact recipe so I made something similar." Though the Haiti-made Barbancourt is a very specific choice, it's the dark, rich buckwheat honey that defines this drink, giving it a cloudy appearance and rangy, full-bodied character. I recommend a large lemon twist.

2 ounces Barbancourt 15-year rum
½ ounce Buckwheat Honey Syrup (see below)
4 dashes Angostura bitters
Lemon twist

Combine all the ingredients except the lemon twist in an Old-Fashioned glass. Add one large chunk of ice and stir until chilled. Twist a large piece of lemon zest over the drink and drop into the glass.

BUCKWHEAT HONEY SYRUP

MAKES ½ CUP

½ cup buckwheat honey
½ cup water

Combine the buckwheat honey and water in a saucepan over low heat. Stir until blended. Remove from the heat and let cool before using. Stored tightly sealed in the refrigerator, the syrup will keep for 1 week.

SORGHUM OLD-FASHIONED

ROBERT NEWTON, SEERSUCKER, BROOKLYN, 2012

The Sorghum Old-Fashioned was the very first cocktail that Robert Newton, owner of the Southern-inspired restaurant Seersucker, developed after receiving a full liquor license. "I wanted to create a drink that was classic and yet spoke to the South and the traditions we explore at the restaurant."

2 ounces Old Overholt rye
¼ ounce Sorghum Syrup (see below)
2 dashes Dutch's colonial cocktail bitters
2 orange twists
Brandied cherry, for garnish

Combine the syrup, bitters, and 1 orange twist in a mixing glass and muddle. Add the rye, fill the glass with ice, and stir until chilled. Strain into a chilled Old-Fashioned glass over a single chunk of ice. Garnish with the other orange twist and the cherry.

SORGHUM SYRUP

MAKES 2 CUPS

1 cup sugar
1 cup sorghum syrup
2 cups water

Combine the sugar, sorghum syrup, and water in a small saucepan and bring to a simmer. Cook, stirring, until the sugar has dissolved. Remove from the heat and let cool before using. Stored tightly sealed in the refrigerator, the syrup will keep for 1 week.

 OLD BAY RIDGE

DAVID WONDRICH, 5 NINTH, NEW YORK CITY, 2005

Wondrich, an early advocate of the old-school Old-Fashioned, created this simple twist on the drink as an homage to the Brooklyn neighborhood of Bay Ridge, which "used to be peopled with Irish folks, who drank rye, and Scandinavians, who drank aquavit." The result is a drink of surprisingly complex spiciness.

1½ ounces Rittenhouse rye

1½ ounces Linie aquavit

1 teaspoon Demerara syrup (page 73)

2 dashes Angostura bitters

Lemon twist

Combine ingredients in Old-Fashioned glass over one large ice cube and stir until chilled. Twist a large piece of lemon zest over the drink and drop into the glass.

THE HIGGINS

DAMIAN HIGGINS, 2012

B etween the funky Smith & Cross Jamaican pot still rum, the maple syrup, and the molasses-tinged blackstrap bitters, this drink might have proved too heavy by half, but it is raised and lifted by that edge-providing pinch of salt. Higgins is not a bartender but a DJ who works under the name Dieselboy.

2 ounces Smith & Cross rum

¼ ounce Grade B maple syrup

2 dashes Bittercube blackstrap bitters

Pinch of salt

Orange twist

Combine all the ingredients except the orange twist in an Old-Fashioned glass. Add one large chunk of ice and stir until chilled. Twist a large piece of orange zest over the drink and drop into the glass.

PERIQUE OLD-FASHIONED

ROBERT SIMONSON, 2013

Perique is a liqueur made from Louisiana perique, a rare tobacco that had been cultivated in St. James Parish for centuries. Made by distiller Ted Breaux, who spearheaded the rebirth of absinthe, it is made in France and, as of this writing, is not available in the United States. However, its arrival is expected imminently. Soft and floral yet intense in flavor and long in finish, a little Perique is all that's needed in this simple Old-Fashioned variation. Going on instinct alone, I reached for New Orleans's own Peychaud's bitters instead of Angostura, and damned if that wasn't the right grace note. Local ingredients stick together. I'd suggest drinking this with an evening cigar. But really, the slightly tannic, palate-drying drink is the cigar itself. Have a glass of ice water handy.

2 ounces Buffalo Trace bourbon
⅛ ounce (about ¾ teaspoon) Perique liqueur
1 sugar cube
2 dashes Peychaud's bitters
Lemon twist

Muddle the sugar, bitters, and a barspoon of warm water at the bottom of an Old-Fashioned glass until the sugar is dissolved. Add the bourbon and Perique and one large chunk of ice and stir until chilled. Twist a large piece of lemon zest over the drink and drop into the glass.

THE BARTENDER

ROBERT SIMONSON, 2013

Given your average modern mixologist's love for both the Old-Fashioned and the bitter Italian *digestivo* Fernet Branca, the name of this drink was a foregone conclusion. This is simply an Old-Fashioned with an extra herbal, menthol punch. It's basically a twist on the Toronto cocktail, except that drink traditionally calls for Canadian whisky and an orange twist, and is served up. I am generally partial to orange twists in my Old-Fashioned, but the extra bite and brightness of a lemon twist is a must here. Given the level of rampant invention in the cocktail community, I have little doubt that this exact drink has already been created by some bartender in some bar somewhere. But that bartender didn't write this book.

---

2 ounces Buffalo Trace bourbon

¼ ounce Fernet Branca

1 sugar cube

2 dashes Angostura bitters

Lemon twist

Muddle the sugar, bitters, and a barspoon of warm water at the bottom of an Old-Fashioned glass until the sugar is dissolved. Add the bourbon and Fernet Branca and one large chunk of ice and stir until chilled. Twist a large piece of lemon zest over the drink and drop into the glass.

ACKNOWLEDGMENTS

MY FIRST AND LARGEST THANKS go to my editor, Emily Timberlake, at Ten Speed Press. Even though she didn't know me, she took up my proposal and fought for it until her superiors (no doubt plied with many an Old-Fashioned) had no choice but to submit. This book exists because she spied, understood, and came to share my passion for a simple drink. Thanks, too, to Daniel Krieger, who, as the best photographer of cocktails I know, was my first choice to photograph the drinks in this book and brought the beauty I expected to its pages.

I am grateful for the generosity of the bartenders and mixologists (and one disc jockey) who allowed their inventions to be printed in this volume: Eric Alperin, Dave Arnold, Anu Apte, Damon Boelte, Tad Carducci, Erick Castro, Frank Cisneros, Eben Freeman, St. John Frizell, Tonia Guffey, Chris Hannah, Bobby Heugel, Damian Higgins, Lynn House, Dustin Knox, Jason Kosmas, Don Lee, Theo Lieberman, Tom Macy, Toby Maloney, Lynnette Marrero, Brian Miller, Robert Newton, Jeremy Oertel, Doug Petry, Julie Reiner, Mike Ryan, Jon Santer, Joaquín Simó, Marcos Tello, Phil Ward, and David Wondrich. I've met all but a couple of you, I've been on the receiving end of your skills. You are artists all.

Thanks, also, to Brad Thomas Parsons, who introduced me to Emily Timberlake without having actually met me first; Dale DeGroff and Brian Rea, who shared their memories of tending bar in the New York during the golden and not-so-golden years of the late twentieth century; my mother, for sharing her memories of drinking during those years; cocktail historian David Wondrich, who shared his vast knowledge of drinking history and a few critical newspaper clippings and made a present of my personal grail, an actual Old-Fashioned spoon; Greg Boehm, for the use of his comprehensive library of cocktail books, his collection of cocktail glasses, and for providing the image of Theodore Proulx; Christina Clum and the folks at Cointreau, for access to their collection of old cocktail manuals; the kind and helpful staff of the New York Public Library, particularly its Carroll Gardens, Brooklyn, branch; musician and music historian Michael Feinstein, for providing the lyrics to "A Good Old-Fashioned Cocktail (with a Good Old-Fashioned Gal)"; Jennifer DeBolt, the owner of Madison's bar and restaurant The Old Fashioned; the Pendennis Club; the staff of Louisville's Filson Historical Society; Bourbon distiller Trey Zoeller; Ellen Keith at the Chicago History Museum Research Center, for going above and beyond the call of duty; Bopkat Vintage and barman Del Pedro, for the loan of their vintage glassware; Fort Defiance, Prime Meats, Donna, The Butterfly, Arnaud's, and especially Maison Premiere, for the use of their beautiful bars as photo backdrops, and to those bars' bartenders, beverage directors, and owners, St. John Frizell, Damon Boelte, Jeremy Oertel, Eben Freeman, Chris Hannah, and Maxwell Britten, respectively, for helping build the drinks seen in those pictures.

Thank you Heaven Hill for making Elijah Craig and Henry McKenna bourbon, and Rittenhouse rye. You make making a good Old-Fashioned easy.

Lastly, thanks and much love to my wife Sarah and son Asher for their support and encouragement.

INDEX

ABOUT THE AUTHOR

ROBERT SIMONSON writes about drinks, drink makers, drink servers, and drinking establishments for the *New York Times.* His family doesn't understand his job and worries about him. His friends do understand his job and wonder how he got it. His wife thinks there are too many bottles in their apartment and wants him to rent a storage space. His writings have also appeared in *Wine Spectator, Wine Enthusiast, Imbibe, Edible* (Manhattan, Brooklyn, Queens, and East End versions), the now-defunct *New York Sun, Saveur, Whisky Advocate,* and the food blog *Eater,* where he wrote a column called "A Beer At" until he couldn't stand one more pint at one more Irish pub. He lives with his wife and son in the Carroll Gardens section of Brooklyn, about equidistant between Fort Defiance and Clover Club, if you know those bars. The Old-Fashioned really is his favorite drink.